Excavation of the Donner-Reed Wagons

Excavation of the Donner-Reed Wagons: Historic Archaeology Along the Hastings Cutoff

by

Bruce R. Hawkins and David B. Madsen

with contributions by

Ann Hanniball

Brigham D. Madsen

M. Elizabeth Manion

Gary Topping

Illustrations by Bruce R. Hawkins

THE UNIVERSITY OF UTAH PRESS

Salt Lake City

Copyright © 1990 The University of Utah Press

Paperback edition 1999
ISBN 0-87480-605-4

Hardcover edition previously cataloged as:

Hawkins, Bruce R.
  Excavation of the Donner-Reed wagons : historic archaeology along
the Hastings Cutoff / by Bruce R. Hawkins and David B. Madsen,
with contributions by Ann Hanniball . . . [et al.] ; illustrations by Bruce
R. Hawkins.
      p.   cm.
  Includes bibliographical references.

  1. Great Salt Lake Desert (Utah) – Antiquities. 2. Donner Party.
3. Wagons – Utah – Great Salt Lake Desert. 4. Excavations
(Archaeology) – Utah – Great Salt Lake Desert. I. Madsen,
David B.
II. Title.
F832.G7H38   1990
979.2'43 – dc20   89-20129
                                                      CIP

Contents

Illustrations and Tables

Preface

Excavations of the Donner-Reed wagons were undertaken as part of a series of archaeological surveys and excavations conducted over a span of 5 years, from 1983 to 1988, by the Antiquities Section of the Utah State Historical Society. These projects were focused on an area west of the Great Salt Lake around the playa of the Great Salt Lake Desert. They have jointly come to be called the Silver Island Expedition since most of the work involved both historic and prehistoric sites in and along the Silver Island Range east of the Utah/Nevada border.

The projects were undertaken for a variety of reasons, ranging from strict research interests to evaluations required by federal-state land exchanges to mitigation efforts necessitated by large development projects. Funding to support these projects was equally varied, ranging from National Science Foundation Grant #BNS-8607545 to federal land management monies to state water resource funds. Despite the apparent diversity of this survey and excavation program, the work of the Silver Island Expedition was essentially coherent and revolved around a central theme—investigation of human adaptation in and adaptability to the harsh environments of the Great Salt Lake deserts.

The Donner-Reed excavations were specifically undertaken as part of a salvage effort necessitated by the construction of a water impoundment on the Great Salt Lake Desert. During the 1980s, the Great Salt Lake reached and exceeded its historic high, flooding many features along the lake edge and endangering many more. A pumping project designed to move these rising lake waters into evaporation ponds on the western Utah deserts was conceived and executed in 1986, and this necessitated the excavation of the remains of several emigrant wagons which would be disturbed by pond construction.

While each of the major projects of the Silver Island Expedition are presented separately, a major portion of the research is integrated by an investigative framework aimed at defining the behavior of prehistoric hunting and gathering peoples who occupied the caves of western Utah. This research is currently being prepared as a separate subset of the *University of Utah Anthropological Papers*. The present volume stands somewhat apart, and is being presented in a different format, because it deals with the archaeological investigation of a tiny fraction of a large, complex, midnineteenth-century industrial society. This different focus necessarily involved different research questions and even different archaeological techniques (such as the use of an English rather than a metric mapping system). As a result, we have attempted to make this report of the historic archaeology of the Hastings Cutoff and the Donner-Reed wagons self-contained and internally whole rather than integrate it fully with the hunter-gatherer studies. Nevertheless, the research reported in this volume does share a number of features with the rest of our work (not the least of which was the misery of working out on the salt flats in the midst of a northern Great Basin winter), and reference to these other studies may be appropriate.

Acknowledgments

The many individuals and institutions who generously contributed time, energy, and resources toward the completion of this report are due special thanks. Financial support was provided by the Utah Division of Water Resources. Fieldwork was performed principally by Bruce Hawkins, James Kirkman, and Gary Topping, Utah Division of State History. John Grossnickle and members of the 2701st EOD Squadron, Hill Air Force Base, provided significant field assistance. Paul Summers and Clark Ogden of the Utah Division of Water Resources were particularly helpful in making logistics arrangements. Utah Department of Transportation Maintenance Station 221, Wendover, Utah, provided storage space for tools and equipment. The Utah National Guard arranged for helicopter support.

Foremost among those who provided laboratory and analytical support were Dr. Phil Fredricks and the staff of the LDS Hospital Radiology Department. Without the help of the X rays which they generously provided, the identification of iron specimens, which formed the bulk of the recovered artifacts, would not have been possible. Others who provided laboratory and analytical support include James Madsen, Utah Division of State History, who shared his laboratory facilities and identified geological specimens, and pinpointed their source areas. Ferris Allgood of the USDA Soil Conservation Service provided a description and analysis of the soils which formed the stratigraphy of the sites. Brooke Bowman, Fort Douglas Museum, provided advice on the cleaning and treatment of textile and leather artifacts. Ann Hanniball, Utah Museum of Natural History, performed the analysis of textile specimens. Mary Elizabeth Manion, Utah Division of State History, identified faunal remains. Richard Fike, Bureau of Land Management, identified patent/proprietary medicine containers. Richard Fischer, Department of Forest Resources, Utah State University, identified wood fragments.

Numerous individuals patiently provided access to museums, frequently on short notice. Ruth Matthews, Grantsville, Utah, provided access to study the collection at the Donner-Reed Memorial Museum on numerous occasions. This collection acquired largely in the 1930s forms perhaps the best collection of artifacts from Hastings Cutoff in the United States. Warren Beers allowed the authors to examine wagon parts and accession records at the Emigrant Museum, Donner Memorial State Park, Truckee, California. Ron Brentano, Oregon Historical Society, answered endless questions and allowed us to make notes and sketches of specimen no. 2659, a light farm wagon with 1845 provenience to the Oregon Trail. Martha Frankel and Marty West of the Lane County Historical Museum, Eugene, Oregon, also answered countless questions and allowed us to make notes and sketches of two wagons and other artifacts with Oregon Trail provenience in their collection. Donald Hardesty, University of Nevada-Reno, and Betty Graham Lee, Safford, Arizona, thoroughly reviewed the manuscript and provided a number of useful suggestions. Renae Hendry, Utah Division of State History, typed the manuscript and efficiently attended to the many administrative details which kept the project on line and solvent.

ONE

Introduction

The tragic fate of the Donner-Reed party of California emigrants is one of the most famous episodes in the history of western expansion and settlement. The party's late arrival in the Sierra Nevada Mountains caused it to be stranded by snow during the winter of 1846–47 and led to starvation and the death of much of the party. Unfortunately, the lurid tales of cannibalism associated with this winter camp in the Sierra have tended to obscure the rest of the Donner-Reed story. What is less well known is that the tragedy of the Donner party's experience in the Sierra was caused in large part by the delays and difficulties which they encountered while crossing the Wasatch Mountains and the Great Salt Lake Desert in Utah. Delays caused by cutting a new trail through Emigration Canyon east of Salt Lake City, together with the loss of at least four wagons and numerous oxen in the mud of the desert playa west of the Great Salt Lake, were primarily responsible for the ultimate demise of the Donner-Reed party.

The Donner-Reed party was just one of numerous emigrant parties to have crossed the continent to California in 1846. Unlike the Donners, however, most groups reached their destination without serious mishap. The members of the Donner-Reed party were affluent midwestern farmers and merchants who began their westward trek late in the season with overloaded and outsized wagons. At the present site of Fort Bridger, Wyoming, the party made a decision to try a new route, largely untested by wagon traffic, pioneered the previous spring by Lansford Hastings, a zealous California promoter. The new trail, referred to as Hastings Cutoff, crossed the Wasatch Mountains and the Great Salt Lake Desert of Utah, "shortening" the standard route to California by 400 miles (Figure 1).

The high sand dunes, soft desert mud, and heat encountered by the Donner-Reed party during their crossing of the waterless 90-mile desert weakened and killed many of the oxen. In an effort to get the thirsty animals to water at springs located along the foot of Pilot Peak in Nevada, the emigrants jettisoned possessions along the route and finally abandoned a number of wagons. So many animals died or wandered off during the crossing that four of the wagons were left behind permanently. One wagon belonging to Lewis Keseberg was left standing in place. The remainder belonging to George Donner and James Reed were supposedly filled with nonessential possessions, covered with boards, and buried as caches.

The mud in which these wagons were supposedly buried is a product of the alternate flooding and desiccation of the western Utah desert as the Great Salt Lake rises and falls with changing climatic cycles. Long-term fluctuations of the lake range on the order of 25 feet at scales of less than 200 years to nearly 40 feet at scales of several thousand years. Over a period of the last 10 years, the current lake fluctuation has been on an upward swing and has been in the process of flooding fixed assets along the lakeshore built when the lake was at a low ebb in the cycle. In order to protect these resources, the State of Utah determined that the most efficient procedure was to transfer water from the main body of the lake, across the Eardley threshold by means of large pumps, to the Great Salt Lake Desert where evaporation could maintain the lake at a fixed level. The West Desert Pumping Project involved the construction of a series of dikes which created an impoundment area between the Newfoundland Mountains on the east and Floating Island on the west. This impoundment area was thought to contain portions of the Hastings Cutoff trail and the remains of four to five wagons abandoned by the Donner-Reed party.

Fifteen recorded and any number of unrecorded expeditions have visited the abandoned wagon sites since 1847, and these existing data suggested that the sites were in an area where they could be destroyed by the pumping project. Members of many of these expeditions collected artifacts and recorded their explorations using both written descriptions and photographs. Using these data, in conjunction with Department of Interior Cadastral Survey field notes, a Hill Air Force Base survey crew under the direction of John Grossnickle

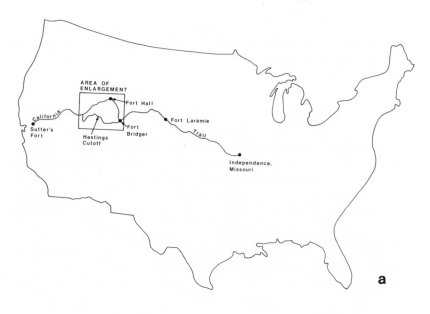

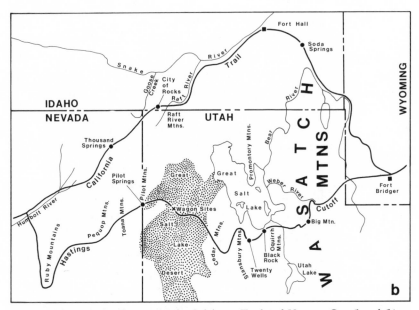

Figure 1. Location map showing (a) the California Trail and Hastings Cutoff, and (b) an enlargement of the research area and the wagon sites along Hastings Cutoff.

located five sites thought to contain the remains of the abandoned wagons. The sites were located along soil discolorations believed to be the wagon wheel ruts of Hastings Cutoff, and were within the boundaries of the Hill Air Force Base north bombing range. Once these sites were identified, it became obvious both (1) that at least portions of the sites remained intact and (2) that they were susceptible to rapid destruction. With the creation of a shallow lake over the sites, it was clear that the combination of the removal of existing salt crust through solution and subsequent wave action of the impounded water would destroy what remained of the buried wagons and their contents.

As a result, a series of consultations between the U.S. Air Force, the National Advisory Council on Historic Preservation, the Utah Division of State History, and the Utah Division of Water Resources over how best to mitigate the potential damage to the sites, led to a decision to initiate archaeological excavations aimed at recovering surviving artifactual remains and the information associated with them. Once this decision was reached, the Antiquities Section of the Division of State History was asked to put together a research design and to excavate what remained of the Donner-Reed wagons. This research design was directed at more than the mere excavation and removal of remaining artifacts, since the sites offered the potential to study the behavior and material culture of midnineteenth-century immigrants, particularly those bound for California. The environment of the sites created the potential for the survival of textiles, leather, and other organic materials not normally encountered in open historic sites. Data obtained from the sites could help in answering such questions as: What can the remains tell us about California emigrants? How many of the items which they transported across the continent did they consider critical to the maintenance of their way of life or cultural traditions? Which items were retained for physical survival when an emigrant faced disaster? Did the goods transported by emigrants across country vary depending on the region from which they came? Were the goods carried by California emigrants different from those carried by Oregon emigrants?

These general questions were put into sharper focus by available historical information reviewed in Chapters 2 through 4, allowing us to add specific questions to our research design. This is perhaps the most exciting aspect of historic archaeology. The combination of written documentation with archaeological excavation techniques allows a more detailed investigation and interpretation of the material remains that are the usual subject matter of archaeological research. At the same time, the detailed examination of physical remains allows a direct assessment of the tall tales, rumors, and myths that tend to collect around well-known historical events such as the Donner-Reed tragedy. Some of the more important of these specific questions were:

1. Have physical remains associated with the Hastings Cutoff trail survived and where are they located?
2. Is there evidence of the trail itself and what is its orientation?
3. Were wagons and cached goods described by James Reed and Virginia Reed Murphy really buried in the mud?
4. What became of the wagons, clothing, tools, and other abandoned items described by Howard Stansbury and other later travelers?
5. What kind of goods were left at the sites and were these remains indeed those abandoned by the Donner-Reed party?
6. Is there any consistency in the kinds of goods that were abandoned?
7. Do rumors of buried gold and precious jewels at the sites have any validity?

The five sites we investigated, 42To467–42To471, are located on the mud flats of the Great Salt Lake Desert approximately 35 miles northeast of Wendover, Nevada, and 130 miles northwest of Salt Lake City, Utah. The sites are between 3.7 and 5.4 miles east-southeast of Floating Island, an isolated eastern extension of the Silver Island Range now surrounded by playa (Figure 2). The sites are located 1/4 to 3/4 miles apart along a southeast to northwest line marked by linear stains in the salt playa surface. The closest site to Floating Island, 42To470, is 101 degrees east of north and 3.7 miles from Floating Island in the northwest quarter of the southwest quarter of Section 22, Township 2 North, Range 15 West. The next site, 42To471, is 122 degrees east of north and 1400 feet from site 42To470. The site is in the southeast quarter of the southwest quarter of Section 22, Township 2 North, Range 15 West. The third site, 42To469, is 122 degrees east of north and 350 feet from site 42To471 in the southeast quarter of the southwest quarter of Section 22, Township 2 North, Range 15 West. The fourth site, 42To468, is 116 degrees and 4650 feet from 42To469. It is in the southwest quarter of the northwest quarter of Section 26, Township 2 North, Range 15 West. The fifth and final site, 42To467, is 128

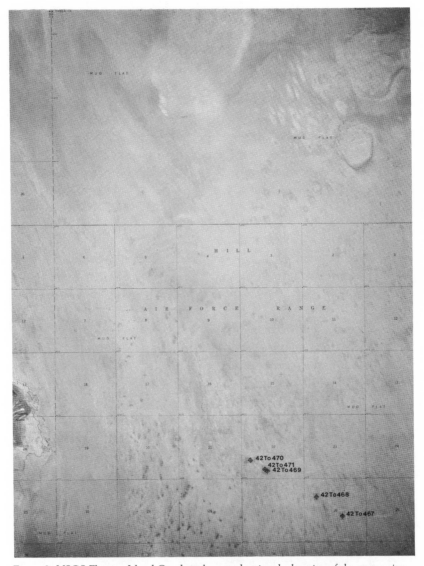

Figure 2. USGS Floating Island Quadrangle map showing the location of the wagon sites.

degrees east of north and 2750 feet from site 42To468 in the north-west quarter of the southeast quarter of Section 26, Township 2 North, Range 15 West.

The mud flats of the Great Salt Lake Desert encompass a 3500-square-mile area of flat featureless terrain. Soils include wind-deposited sediments of sand and silt which have covered the clay loam surface soil and water-deposited subsoils of lake playa clays and silts. The nearest source of fresh water to the sites is at Pilot Springs, Nevada, a distance of 25 miles to the northwest. No floral resources were available for forage within the vicinity of the sites. With the exception of occasional birds which ventured onto the flats after insects, no other signs of faunal resources were observed. This rather prosaic description does no real justice to the desert playa environment where the wagons were found, and early journal accounts are often more illuminating. As one early traveler in the vicinity of the Great Salt Lake put it, "Hell is not one mile from this place." A more recent recounting of Jedediah Smith's 1826 trek across the salt flats is less pointed but more descriptive. The only way Smith and his companions could deal with the heat and aridity of the desert was by digging themselves into the sand during the day as "the sun arose upon this desolate waste which had no end; [and] gleamed upon the sterile salt with a cruel brilliance, [it was] 'insuportably tormenting' " (Morgan 1973:87).

A wide range of climatic conditions were observed and encountered by the project crew between September and December 1986. Extreme daytime heat and thunderstorms which turned the playa into a series of shallow lakes were encountered in September and October. Occasional high windstorms and blowing salt were experienced in October and November. December brought cold temperatures and high winds. The conditions provided the crew in their open vehicles with first-hand knowledge of the conditions and hardships faced by those using this route over 100 years ago.

TWO

Overland Emigration, the California Trail, and the Hastings Cutoff*

Gary Topping

Most of those who have attempted to define an American national character have observed that we are a restless and rootless people. To Frederick Jackson Turner, for example, American democracy itself was a child of the frontier: as Americans moved out into a continent of unclaimed land, there was a natural loosening of the traditional feudal bonds of inherited privilege which created a characteristically American egalitarianism. Others, such as Nathaniel Hawthorne and Alexis de Tocqueville, saw that loosening of social bonds in less optimistic terms as a sort of cultural retrogradation in which Americans threw off valuable traditions and a sense of common purpose. Whatever one wishes to make of it, the existence of vast amounts of available land, particularly as Americans began to move across the Mississippi River during the nineteenth century, was one of the fundamental determinants in shaping our history.

It was the Louisiana Purchase of 1803 that first propelled Americans across the Mississippi, onto the Great Plains, and into the Rocky Mountains. Once begun, the westward movement was inexorable: soon Americans were settling in Texas under special circumstances allowed by the Mexican government, in Oregon's Willamette Valley under the watchful eye of the Hudson's Bay Company's Dr. John McLoughlin, and in the sunny central valleys of California, whence they had been lured from the sea by the hide and tallow trade. Perhaps it was indeed

---

*Part of this chapter appeared in the *Utah Historical Quarterly* 56, no. 2 (Spring 1988): 108–27.

"manifest destiny," as expansionist promoters of the day had it, that the Americans should eventually possess a transcontinental empire, for the small bands of supplicant settlers that first reached foreign soil in each of those areas proved to be only the vanguard of mass migration. In time, the American interlopers surpassed in either numbers or aggressiveness the natives, and by a variety of means, including revolution, as in Texas, or international treaty, as in Oregon, the pilgrims became the possessors. During the mere half century that separates the Louisiana Purchase from the Gadsden Purchase, the United States grew from a minor nation still mainly clustered along the eastern seaboard to a major continental empire.

Possessing it was one thing; populating it was another. In 1803 the only practical means of access to the Pacific Coast was a circuitous and perilous sea voyage. Access to the interior of what became the United States, with the exception of a few Spanish trails in the southwest, was nonexistent beyond the mere fringes. The first reconnaissance of the newly acquired inland empire was the Lewis and Clark expedition of 1804–6. A primary stated purpose of the expedition was, in addition to scientific and diplomatic work, to discover a water route across the continent if in fact one existed. To that end, Lewis and Clark ascended the Missouri River to its headwaters and crossed to the Columbia by means of passes in present-day Montana and Idaho (DeVoto 1953:xv-lii). It was a way across the continent, but it was not adequate for wagons. Discovery of the great pass through the Rocky Mountains that made overland emigration possible was the work of the mountain men who followed hard upon the heels of Lewis and Clark and who accomplished the first thorough geographical investigation of the North American interior.

During the years following the Lewis and Clark expedition, the fur trade along the Missouri and its tributaries became increasingly important, but there were few discoveries during that time that contributed much to the development of a wagon road across the continent. The reason is that the early traders and trappers still operated along the Lewis and Clark route, which was relatively circuitous as a transcontinental crossing, and in addition Indian resistance built constantly until the mountain men began looking for an alternate route after a pitched battle with heavy losses was fought by the Ashley-Henry party of 1823 (Chittenden 1902:262–72). Thereafter, a nearer and easier route to the mountains was developed along the Platte River

(Figure 3), and it was that route that became the main overland trail for emigrants (Mattes 1969).

A small party of men employed by John Jacob Astor returning from the establishment of a trading post on the Columbia River in 1812 were the first white men to use South Pass, the easy and direct route through the Rocky Mountains that more than any other discovery made overland emigration possible. But knowledge of it did not pass into general circulation until it was rediscovered in 1824 by a party of Ashley-Henry men under the great mountain man and explorer Jedediah Smith (Morgan 1953:91–92). Thereafter, though other routes continued to be used, the major access to the Rocky Mountains was up the Platte to the Sweetwater River and up the Sweetwater to South Pass, and it was that route that the overland wagons followed.

It was the missionary Marcus Whitman who took the first wagon through South Pass in 1836. Whitman was a genuine harbinger of emigration: his wife, Narcissa, was the first white woman to cross the Rocky Mountains, and although the fact that he took a wheeled cart all the way to the Columbia that year was more of a stunt than a practical accomplishment, he did demonstrate that the trip was possible, if not yet practical, for families and wagons (Drury 1937:133–54).

And what of those who wished to reach California? Development of a wagon road to California was first attempted in 1841 by the Bartleson-Bidwell party. We are fortunate to have both first-hand and reminiscent accounts of the trip from the pen of one of the principals, John Bidwell, in whose lighthearted prose much of the humor, the frustration, and the improbable spirit of the venture memorably comes alive (Bidwell 1890). Although even more poorly equipped and otherwise unprepared for arduous overland travel than the Donner-Reed party five years later, the Bartleson-Bidwell emigrants somehow succeeded in their journey, becoming the first overland party of settlers to reach California and including the first woman settler to cross the Sierra, Nancy Kelsey (Chiles 1930; Montgomery 1930; Belden 1930).

The story begins with the young man John Bidwell who, at twenty years of age, was suddenly possessed of a desire to see the West. He left his home in western Ohio to catch a boat at Cincinnati for St. Louis and the Missouri frontier with an outfit that was simplicity itself: about seventy-five dollars, a few extra clothes in a knapsack, and formidable armament in the form of a pocketknife. Passing on to the

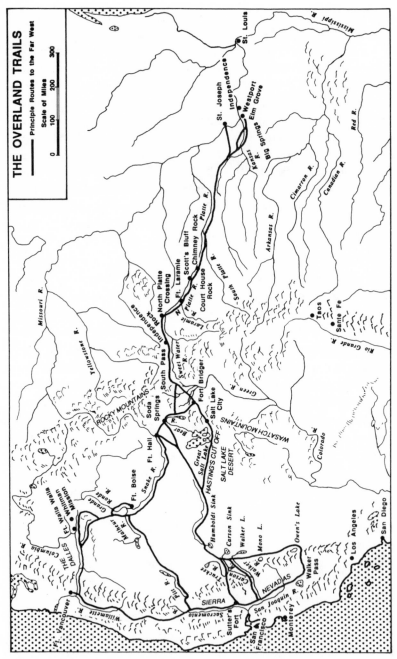

Figure 3. Principal emigrant trails of the western United States (adapted from
Ray Allen Billington, The Far Western Frontier, 1830-1860
[New York: Harper & Bros., 1956], 97).

frontier, he settled on a tract of land recently bought from the Indians and known as the Platte Purchase. Though he was forced to teach school for a time to keep solvent, he was able to acquire 160 acres and to begin making it a habitable home. Unfortunately, while he was on a trip to St. Louis, a man Bidwell calls a bully jumped his claim, and since Bidwell had not yet reached his majority, he was unable to make his claim stick in court.

In the meantime, Bidwell had heard glowing reports of California from a mountain man, and since his prospects in Missouri were dim, he formed a group called the Western Emigration Society, with the purpose of traveling together to California in the spring of 1841. The society attracted initially some five hundred members but, as such things go, only sixty-nine of them actually showed up at the rendezvous in May.

It was an improbable group indeed that assembled for the journey. "Our ignorance of the route was complete," Bidwell admitted. "We knew that California lay west, and that was the extent of our knowledge." A map which one of Bidwell's friends possessed, depicted two rivers emerging from the Great Salt Lake, both larger than the Mississippi, and his friend advised him to plan on building canoes at that point and floating all the way to California. Though they rejected that plan, the equipment they did bring was almost as ineffective as canoes. It would become important later on, for one thing, that some brought mules and horses and others brought oxen, which would mean that the rate of travel would vary considerably between the two groups. All were relatively impoverished: "I doubt whether there was one hundred dollars in money in the whole party," Bidwell recalled, but all were enthusiastic and anxious to go." Bidwell's partner, who was to provide the horses to pull Bidwell's wagon, backed out at the last moment. Bidwell must have been a persuasive salesman though, for he talked another man into throwing in with him and allowing Bidwell to trade a nice black horse he had for a yoke of oxen to draw the wagon and a one-eyed mule for him to ride. A final source of future frustration was provided by the election of John Bartleson, a relatively well-to-do Missourian, as captain. Bidwell disliked him from the first and thought him a poor choice of leaders, but the rest of the party felt they needed him and the extra manpower of his hired helpers, and Bartleson refused to go unless as captain (Bidwell 1890:108–13; Chiles 1930:53).

The Bartleson-Bidwell party enjoyed their first great stroke of good luck in being allowed to begin the journey with a party of three Jesuits under Father Pierre Jean DeSmet, who were on their way to Fort Hall and beyond to work among the Flathead Indians, and guided by the celebrated mountain man Thomas Fitzpatrick. So they were assured of being in good hands for the first long leg of the journey, as Fitzpatrick knew the way and the Indians, and the genial and courageous DeSmet was, by Bidwell's account, a constant inspiring example of meeting inevitable difficulties with good humor (Bidwell 1890:113–14).

Such good fortune was destined to end, though, at Soda Springs, which Fitzpatrick informed the California contingent would be a good separation point for their divergent destinations. At that point, too, half of the Bartleson-Bidwell party decided that prudence was to be found in continuing on to Oregon, where the route was better known and their future less uncertain. Fitzpatrick knew the mountains well, but he knew little of the way to California, so as the now drastically reduced remainder of the Bartleson-Bidwell party slowly wended off in a southwesterly direction, they instructed four of their men to continue on with the main party to Fort Hall to try to get better information.

The information they got was neither very specific nor very encouraging: "They brought the information that we must strike out west of Salt Lake . . . being careful not to go too far south, lest we should get into a waterless country without grass. They also said we must be careful not to go too far north, lest we should get into a broken country and steep canons, and wander about, as trapping parties had been known to do, and become bewildered and perish" (Bidwell 1890:122). Following directions like those was not easy, and accordingly the party wandered around in the salt desert to the north and west of the Great Salt Lake for some days with no good idea of what they were trying to accomplish and gradually running out of water and provisions.

After blundering across the salt flats, they arrived at the foot of the Pequop Mountains, where they made the fortunate decision that the wagons were too poorly suited for travel on that terrain and should be abandoned in favor of packing what possessions they could on the animals. The emigrants were almost totally ignorant of packing techniques, but they had observed the pack saddles of mountain men along the Green River, and imitated them as best they could with parts fashioned from the wagons. The results, according to Bidwell, were quite inept and humorous, primarily because even the oxen had to carry pack saddles, and their backs were not as suited to them as the horses: "the difficulties we had at first were simply indescribable. . . . It was but a few minutes before the packs began to turn; horses became scared, mules kicked, oxen jumped and bellowed, and articles were scattered in all directions. We took more pains, fixed things, made a new start, and did better, though packs continued occasionally to fall off and delay us" (Bidwell 1890:123).

It was a comical and clumsy way to travel, but it brought them down the Humboldt River, which they followed because of its mediocre supply of water for the animals and its apparently correct direction of flow toward their destination, until it finally gave out in the marshes known as the Humboldt Sink.

Upon reaching the Sierra, though, friction which had developed between the horsemen and owners of oxen finally flared up and produced a division in the party, the more fleet horsemen deciding to let the oxen plod along at their own deliberate rate, while they struck out more rapidly for California. It was an unfortunate decision for Bartleson, the leader of the horsemen, for they missed the pass used by the rest of the party and had to subsist on bad food for some days until they could reunite with the slower contingent. Bidwell reports that food poisoning reduced Bartleson, who was a heavy man, to half his weight, and caused him to swear that "If I ever get back to Missouri I will never leave that country. I would gladly eat out of the troughs with my dogs." And Bidwell wryly adds, "But that did not prevent him from leaving us twice after that" (Bidwell 1890:128).

At the expense of considerable difficulty, indeed suffering, the Bartleson-Bidwell party followed up the Walker River to an arduous crossing of the Sierra to the headwaters of the Stanislaus River and thence down into the San Joaquin Valley to the ranch of Dr. John B. Marsh on November 4, 1841. Although they had succeeded in their quest, their route was not again followed closely across the northern part of the Great Salt Lake Desert, nor across the Sierra. But they had proven that wagons could be taken at least most of the way to California, and perhaps with more exploration a route could be worked out the rest of the way.

It could, as things turned out, but not for a while yet. No attempt was made on the overland route to California in 1842, though the

Elijah White party of Oregon immigrants that year brought Lansford W. Hastings to the Pacific. Finding less than a hearty welcome in Fort Vancouver, Hastings led a party of other disgruntled Oregonians to California the following year and lavished his promotional genius from then on upon California.

In 1843 Joseph B. Chiles, who had been a member of the Bartleson-Bidwell party, returned to the East and organized another wagon train of emigrants bound for California. Aware of the obvious fact that the Bartleson-Bidwell route could be improved upon, he enlisted the services of the mountain man Joseph Reddeford Walker, who had discovered the pass through the Sierra that bears his name, and thought that wagons could be taken through it.

Chiles's first innovation was to avoid the salt flats north of the Great Salt Lake that had so taxed and bewildered the Bartleson-Bidwell party. Instead, he continued along the Oregon Trail to Ft. Boise, where the party divided. Chiles, with a party of one hundred horsemen, ascended the Malheur River and crossed into the upper Sacramento River Valley. The wagon contingent, under Walker, reached the Humboldt, followed it to the Sierra, then turned southward all the way to Owens Valley, where he relocated Walker Pass. They were forced to abandon their wagons in the mountains, however, which proved to be a good move anyway after they reached the San Joaquin Valley and had to struggle through miles of choking alkaline dust before they finally arrived at Sutter's Fort (Stewart 1962:203–7, Billington 1956:98).

By the beginning of the 1844 emigration season, then, two prominent facts characterized the California Trail: it was obvious in the first place that the Humboldt River was indeed, as Dale Morgan has called it, the "highroad of the West." Though it was the most hated of all western rivers, Morgan continued, because of its hostile Indians and brackish, cholera-carrying water, it was also the most necessary, for it pointed the way most directly to the only practical passes over the Sierra (Morgan 1943:5). The other prominent fact was that only pack animals so far had been taken over those mountains, and a wagon road was necessary to sustain any large emigration.

It was the Stevens-Townsend-Murphy party of that year that first crossed what became more or less the standard California Trail and located a pass suitable for wagons through the Sierra. The party is named for the three captains of the eleven wagons, but credit for the route goes largely to the guiding skills of the old mountain man

Caleb Greenwood, who was eighty years old when he left Missouri in March at the head of the emigrant train (Kelly 1936:50–80).

Among Greenwood's accomplishments as guide on that trip was the successful first attempt of the sixty-mile dry shortcut between South Pass and the Green River that became known as the Greenwood Cutoff. The Stevens-Townsend-Murphy party was well equipped with good wagons, light loads, and powerful animals, and so negotiated the stretch with little difficulty. It was later used as a standard alternative on the Oregon Trail by parties similarly well off, though avoided by more poorly equipped groups.

From Fort Hall, Greenwood chose the most logical route to the Humboldt, a route that had not been used before: from Raft River through the City of Rocks, down Goose Creek, across to Bishop Creek, and down it to the Humboldt. How Greenwood knew of the route is uncertain. He claimed to have been in California eighteen years before, and perhaps it was on that trip that he had discovered what turned out to be the most practical wagon route from Fort Hall to the Humboldt. Whatever his previous experience, it is clear that he knew what he was doing. During the subsequent history of the California Trail, only two significant revisions of Greenwood's route through the Great Basin were ever used: the Hastings Cutoff across the salt flats to the south and west of the Great Salt Lake, of which more will be said later, and the Salt Lake Cutoff, which allowed emigrants to use Salt Lake City as a way station, then skirt the Great Salt Lake to the north, passing near present-day Snowville and west to the City of Rocks, where it joined the Greenwood route.

Upon reaching the Humboldt Sink, however, Old Greenwood's knowledge ran out. If he had crossed the mountains before, he had not done so by means of a route that would admit wagons, and so a quest for such a route began. He was fortunate at that time to encounter a Paiute Indian named Truckee, who told him that a river (which now bears the Indian's name) directly to the west of their camp would lead them to a pass that wagons could negotiate. It proved to be a rough pass, but the Indian was right, though the party barely beat the early snows to reach Sacramento.

Three members of the party, in fact, almost did not make it. When the going got rough in the pass, they abandoned two wagons near what came to be called Donner Lake. Since the wagons contained valuable goods that their owners were reluctant to leave to the Indians and the elements, Joseph Foster, Allen Montgomery, and Moses

Schallenberger remained to salvage what they could. The three were caught in the snow and decided to build a cabin and wait out the winter. Finally the first two made a desperate attempt to cross the summit and succeeded, while Schallenberger gave up and returned to the cabin, presumably to die. By a fortunate turn of fate, however, he subsisted on foxes through the winter and was rescued in the spring. The Stevens-Townsend-Murphy party had all reached Sacramento Valley, though only barely and luckily so. But most importantly for the future, the California Trail had been established, the first wagons had reached Sutter's Fort, and the way was now prepared for emigrants. All that remained was the need for a good propagandist to advertise the new route and the glories of California.

Lansford W. Hastings is so deeply rooted in the historiography of the California Trail as the villain in the Donner tragedy that some space needs to be devoted to the exact nature of his role in luring the Donners to the West, and then to the trail that caused their demise. The anti-Hastings historiography began with Charles Kelly's *Salt Desert Trails* (1930), was further developed in George R. Stewart's *Ordeal by Hunger* (1936), and reached its apogee in Bernard DeVoto's *The Year of Decision: 1846* (1943). According to DeVoto's interpretation, Hastings was a recklessly ambitious land speculator with grandiose political ambitions who, in his haste to populate California with Americans to whom he could sell land and lead to secession from Mexico, promoted perilous or impassable trails he had never personally seen. His descriptions of California were so appealing and his knowledge of the routes to it so assuring that the Donners were duped into following his incompetent lead and paid for their naivete with their lives.

DeVoto heaps upon Hastings all the imprecations left over from his excoriation of John C. Frémont; in fact, he calls Hastings "a Frémont in miniature"—no compliment in the DeVoto demimonde of western charlatans (DeVoto 1943:45). He imputes to Hastings motives he never had and events that never occurred, as in his story that Hastings at one point visited Texas to observe there the republic that Sam Houston had created, as a possible model for one he wanted to establish in California. Even more importantly, DeVoto zigzags through Hastings's book like an errant bumblebee, bypassing all its useful advice and landing on its inaccuracies.

There is no question that Hastings's *Emigrants' Guide* is as much an advertising tract as a geographical treatise, nor does Hastings deny the fact. The California one finds in its pages is a paradise in which

"December is as pleasant as May," where disease is virtually unknown, where meat can be cured in its pure atmosphere for weeks without rotting, where wild oats with stalks suitable for walking sticks can be cultivated merely by fencing off a field of them to keep the animals out (Hastings 1845:83, 87; Andrews 1970). And so on.

For the politically ambitious, Hastings indicated that California was ripe for the picking. The Mexicans and Indians who made up the bulk of the population were almost equally ignorant and degraded, and governed despotically by priests and dictators. "A Mexican always pursues that method of doing things which requires the least physical or mental exorcise [sic]," Hastings alleges, "unless it involves some danger, in which case, he always adopts some other method." The purpose of the Catholic Church in California, he continues, was "not only to enslave and oppress, thousands of these timid and unsuspecting aborigines, but also to reduce all of the common, and lower orders, of the people, to a most abject state of vassalage, and to stamp indellible [sic] ignorance and superstition, upon their imbecile and uncultivated minds." Militarily, California was a pushover:

> It was defended by soldiers who are mere Indians, many of whom, are as perfectly wild and untutored, as the most barbarous savages of the forest; yet it is with these wild, shirtless, earless and heartless creatures, headed by a few timid, soulless, brainless officers, that these semi-barbarians, intend to hold this delightful region, as against the civilized world (Hastings 1845:93–94, 105, 122).

In evaluating Hastings's experience as a guide and knowledge of the overland routes, DeVoto is once again selective, emphasizing what Hastings did not know and ignoring what he did. Hastings was in fact a man of considerable outdoor skill, experience, and leadership ability who was able to communicate those qualities to those whom he proposed to guide and, as it turned out, was able to deliver upon his promises. Hastings's overland experience began in 1842 when he joined, and eventually took over leadership of, the Oregon-bound train of Elijah White. After Dr. John McLoughlin, the Hudson's Bay Company factor at Fort Vancouver, discouraged Hastings from settling there and luring even more Americans to follow him, he led another party of equally disgruntled emigrants down the coast to Sacramento. From there he crossed the Sierra twice, perhaps foolishly, in adverse weather and crossed on horseback the cutoff he proposed to lead wagons over in 1846.

With regard to this proposed cutoff, which left the main trail at Fort Bridger, crossed the Wasatch Mountains, and passed to the south of the Great Salt Lake and over the salt flats to rejoin the California Trail at the Humboldt River, DeVoto is most unfair. Hastings's book did not advocate use of that route: it is presented, as Hastings's biographer points out, in an offhanded manner as a geographical observation rather than a suggestion:

> The most direct route, for the California emigrants, would be to leave the Oregon route, about two hundred miles east from Fort Hall; thence bearing west southwest, to the Salt Lake; and thence continuing down to the bay of San Francisco, by the route just described. The emigrants, up to this time, however, have traveled together, as far as Fort Hall, because of this being the only settlement, in that vicinity, at which they are enabled to procure horses, and provisions (Hastings 1845:137–38).

It was only after Hastings had passed across the cutoff himself that he proposed to lead others across it. Indeed it proved to be an extremely difficult route, much more difficult than Hastings had imagined, but Hastings himself successfully led a wagon train over it in 1846, and it was used repeatedly through 1850. DeVoto emphasizes the fact that the mountain man James Clyman, whom DeVoto adopted as his particular hero, passed over the new cutoff with Hastings in 1846 and warned Hastings's "victims," whom Hastings proposed to guide over the trail, to stick to the older route. DeVoto's oblique reference, of course, is to the Donner tragedy as evidence that Clyman was right. In this, however, Clyman was clearly wrong: wagons did successfully use the cutoff—in 1846 and later years. Many who used the route seem to have considered its mileage saving as of Pyrrhic value, given the toll it exacted on people, animals, and equipment; but the Donners, with one exception, were the only ones to lose lives because of it (Kelly 1952b:49).

Hastings himself certainly did not regard the cryptic reference to the cutoff in his *Guide* as sufficient information for emigrants, for he and his partner, the mountain man James Hudspeth, proceeded eastward from Fort Bridger in the summer of 1846 to meet the emigrant parties and offer to guide them through the new route. Finding that they were yet a little early to meet the wagons, the two men decided to take advantage of the fortunate circumstance of a meeting with one Wales Bonney, who was journeying alone from Oregon eastward, and would soon encounter the emigrant parties. Hastings gave Bonney a letter to circulate among the emigrants, advising them to meet him at Fort Bridger, and to consolidate their forces under his leadership to attempt the new cutoff (Korns 1951, Morgan 1963).

The first party to take advantage of Hastings's offer was the Bryant-Russell group who were traveling somewhat in advance of the others because they were on muleback. Edwin Bryant's journal of the trip, published later as *What I Saw in California*, is one of the classics of western narrative (Bryant 1848). A medical doctor who chose a career in journalism, Bryant was on his way from Kentucky to California primarily to write a book about his experiences rather than to settle in the promised land. His partner was William H. Russell, a Kentucky colonel who started out as leader of the party but proved unequal to the task and was replaced. At that point, Bryant, Russell, and seven others decided to sell their wagons and buy mules.

While Hastings decided at Fort Bridger to take charge of the slower wagon parties, the Bryant-Russell group pushed on under the leadership of Hudspeth, who promised to accompany them as far as the salt flats, at which point he intended to leave them to engage in further exploration. Although the Bryant-Russell party left Fort Bridger on July 20, the same day as the polyglot wagon party known as the Harlan-Young group, which was under Hastings's leadership, they soon moved far in advance. Hudspeth elected to lead them across the Wasatch through Weber Canyon, which was a narrow gorge that required frequent riding through the stream, but was otherwise not a difficult passage for animals. The rest of the journey until they parted company with Hudspeth presented no difficulties either. That parting occurred at the summit of Hastings Pass through the Cedar Mountains, from which a long view of the salt flats confronted them. At that point, Bryant reported, Hudspeth gave his final instructions:

> Standing on one of the peaks, he stretched out his long arms, and with a voice and gesture as loud and impressive as he could make them, he called to us and exclaimed—'Now, boys, put spurs to your mules and ride like h_____!' The hint was timely given and well meant, but scarcely necessary, as we all had a pretty just appreciation of the trials and hardships before us (Korns 1951:85–86).

Although Bryant's account contains a fairly forlorn assessment of their prospects at that point, emphasizing the fact that they would have no guide until they struck the California Trail some two hundred miles to the west, they actually were in fairly good condition to meet the challenges of that difficult passage. Their great advantage, of course, was that they had no wagons to worry about. They had a pretty good idea, too, of their course and the nature of the terrain from conversations with Walker, Clyman, Hastings, and Hudspeth, all of whom had considerable familiarity with the country. Even at that, Bryant's initial impression of the salt flats was intimidating:

> From the western terminus of this ominous-looking passage [the Grayback Hills] we had a view of the vast desert-plain before us, which, as far as the eye could penetrate, was of a snowy whiteness, and resembled a scene of wintry frosts and icy desolation. Not a shrub or object of any kind rose above the surface for the eye to rest upon. The hiatus in the animal and vegetable kingdoms was perfect. It was a scene which excited mingled emotions of admiration and apprehension (Korns 1951:85–86).

Bryant's account of their crossing of the salt flats is memorable. Not only did their animals sink at times clear to their bellies in the soft ground, but mirages repeatedly plagued their riders with visions of ethereal cities "with countless columned edifices of marble whiteness, and studded with domes, spires, and turreted towers, [which] would rise upon the horizon of the plain, astonishing us with its stupendous grandeur and sublime magnificence" (Korns 1951:88). Even with those problems, which sometimes forced the riders to dismount, the party eventually reached the springs at Pilot Peak late at night; they had crossed the entire eighty miles in one long day.

The crossing of the salt flats was the only real adventure for the Bryant-Russell party. They had little difficulty in reaching the main California Trail at the Humboldt, and followed the route of the Stevens-Townsend-Murphy party through the Sierra, though they seem to have been unaware of their predecessors' identity or history. They found Schallenberger's cabin at Donner Lake, for instance, but were unaware of its origin.

In terms of overland emigration, the Bryant-Russell party was relatively insignificant, since of its innovations, the route down the Weber as yet disclosed none of the difficulties it would present to wagons, and the Great Salt Lake Desert had been crossed on horseback several times before. It was the Harlan-Young party which followed hard on the heels of the Bryant-Russell group that put the Hastings Cutoff to its first real test.

The Harlan-Young party was a loosely affiliated group of forty wagons which did not really exist as a unit until it left Fort Bridger. Originally a part of the Bryant-Russell party, the Harlan-Young contingent split off when the party was first being organized, giving reasons of compactness and efficiency as their motives. Eventually the party grew to about fifty-seven wagons, as latecomers joined between Fort Bridger and the valley of the Great Salt Lake.

The Weber Canyon route was Hudspeth's choice, not Hastings's. Hudspeth rode back from the Bryant-Russell camp at the mouth of the canyon to convince the Harlan-Young party to follow them down the Weber. Hastings was not with the Harlan-Young group at the time, having ridden back to look after stragglers. By the time he rejoined the party, they were already well into Weber Canyon. The upper part of the canyon was not bad, but the lower reaches presented serious difficulties, necessitating the use of winches for both animals and wagons at some points. It was thus quite probable, in Hastings's mind, that a better route could be found, perhaps present-day Parley's Canyon, which Hastings and Clyman had used to get out of Salt Lake Valley on their earlier trip, and which he probably had intended to try before Hudspeth persuaded the emigrants to try the Weber.

Having crossed the Wasatch, the first great obstacle of the Hastings Cutoff, the emigrants then faced the Great Salt Lake Desert, the other great obstacle. They were not, as we have seen, the first wagon train to have crossed that desert, but they were the first to attempt a crossing to the south of the Great Salt Lake. The crossing took three days, August 16–18, and was extremely trying. Heinrich Lienhard's detachment was the only wagon party to have crossed the Hastings Cutoff through 1850 without having to abandon wagons or animals, but even he complained of great tribulation: "Our oxen all appeared to be suffering; the whole of their bowels appeared to cry out, an incessant rumbling which broke out from all; they were hollow-eyed, and it was most distressing to see the poor animals suffer thus." Lienhard also relates a pathetic story of the oxen pulling his personal wagon, which was second in line. His animals, he said, were in constant danger of breaking off their horns because they were desperate to get too close to the wheels of the first wagon in order to stand briefly in its shade. The other detachments of the Harlan-Young party were less fortunate than Lienhard and his companions: before reaching Pilot Peak, Lienhard counted no less than twenty-four abandoned wagons (about one-third of their total vehicles) on the salt flats (Korns

1951:148–52). The Harlan-Young party lost a number of animals, but abandoned none of the wagons permanently, for they were able to return, with freshly fed and watered animals, to pick up the equipment they had left behind.

The Hastings Cutoff, then, was a usable route, but not a very desirable one. It required light wagons lightly loaded, fresh, strong animals, and a great deal of manpower for hacking trails and winching gear over precipices. The Harlan-Young party made the journey, but at the expense of considerable hardship, and only barely even at that. The Donners were not so fortunate.

If ever a party was doomed at the beginning, it was the Donners (Stewart 1936). The party consisted of eighty-seven people in twenty wagons. Of their total number, only twenty-nine were men fifteen years of age or older who could be expected to perform the hard work of road building in rough country; the rest were women, children, or elderly men. Their equipment was equally inadequate for the purpose, primarily because of James Frazier Reed's "Pioneer Palace" wagon, a two-story behemoth of far too great size and weight, which Reed obstinately refused to abandon until the party reached the Humboldt River. Furthermore, they were intellectually and psychologically unprepared for the trials they would face. They were Illinois farmers who had never seen a mountain or a desert and had no idea how to cope with either except for what they had read in Hastings's *Guide*, and that they had ignored. They were personally incompatible, so that rivalries and hostilities were a constant fact of their social life: Reed and Keseberg feuded; Reed and Snyder fought, resulting in Snyder's murder; Breen refused food to the destitute Eddy family; old man Hardcoop was abandoned to die of exposure—and so on. Finally, they decided for some unknown reason very early on that they would attempt the Hastings Cutoff, even before Hastings himself recommended it as a practical route. James Clyman met Reed as far east as Fort Laramie and reported Reed's intention already to follow the "nigher route" described in Hastings's *Guide*. Unfortunately, they were too late on the trail and too slow to make up the difference, so they deprived themselves of the immediate guide services of Hastings himself, perhaps the one man on the trail at that time who could have brought them through, and of the added manpower available in the Harlan-Young party.

* * *

If history does not disclose its alternatives, still it is difficult to avoid asking what might have happened if Hudspeth had taken the Harlan-Young party through Parley's Canyon instead of the Weber, which Hastings recognized the Donners simply could not have negotiated with their limited manpower. A usable road would already have existed for the Donners, thus eliminating the need for the extremely taxing and time-consuming trail hacking through Emigration Canyon. Or what if Reed had been induced to abandon his Pioneer Palace early in the mountains, and the others had been able to catch up with the Harlan-Young party and gone down the Weber with them instead?

The Donner-Reed party arrived in Fort Bridger on July 27, 1846, only a week after the Bryant-Russell and Harlan-Young parties had left, but they had been driving their animals so hard to get there that they stayed four more days to allow them to rest and recuperate. By the time they left, on July 31, they were thus eleven days behind the others, and thus out of reach of any real assistance. The gap widened as the summer and fall continued, and the weather in the Sierra would not wait.

The Donner wagons had no trouble following their predecessors to the head of Weber Canyon, but when they got there, they found a note from Hastings advising against that route and offering to return to help them find another if they would send a messenger ahead to get him. Unfortunately, by the time Reed and two others could get to Hastings, he was already at Adobe Rock in Tooele Valley and was no longer in a position to guide them personally through the Wasatch. Instead, he returned with Reed to the summit of Big Mountain, where he pointed out an alternative route, which the Donner-Reed party then followed. The alternative was arduous in the extreme, indeed almost beyond the ability of the party, but at least it was passable to them, which the Weber was not.

The delay in getting through the Wasatch was great, as was the toll on their animals. For many days in getting through East Canyon and over to Mountain Dell, they made only two or three miles, hacking every inch of the way through the tangled brush, and double- and triple-teaming their wagons over the hills. Where the Harlan-Young party had taken eighteen days to get from Fort Bridger to the valley of the Great Salt Lake (July 20–August 7), it took the Donners twenty-six days (July 27–August 22). Even more to the point, perhaps, is the fact that on August 22, when the Donners emerged from Emigration

Canyon, the Harlan-Young party was resting their animals at Pilot Spring, having crossed the last of the unknown and formidable obstacles of the Hastings Cutoff.

It took the Donner-Reed party three days, August 31 to September 2, to cross the salt flats, and the effect of the crossing on their animals, equipment, and morale was devastating. The Donner animals were much less prepared for the arduous crossing than had been the Harlan-Young animals, so it is no wonder that they, too, began to fail long before the passage was completed. Many of their animals simply died on the spot before water could be brought back for them, or wandered off to die or possibly to fall into the hands of Indians. Two of Reed's three wagons had to be abandoned on the salt flats, as did one of George Donner's and one of Lewis Keseberg's.

The nature of the wagon caches and exactly what was left behind has been the source of some confusion in subsequent literature. The confusion mainly springs from Virginia Reed's after-the-fact account, in which she claims that her father placed the two wagons in holes in the ground and covered them up, after having placed in them all the goods to be abandoned. One of the wagons, she asserts, was the Pioneer Palace (Korns 1951:214). None of this is true. Virginia Reed, along with the rest of her family, had been taken to Pilot Springs, where they remained while the men returned to make the caches, so she could not have witnessed the process and thus reported it wrongly. As will be seen in Chapter 6, nothing was buried at the sites of the abandoned wagons; the mounds discovered there by early salvagers were simply sand and salt blown against the wagon boxes. And it is a mystery how she could have reported that the Pioneer Palace was one of the abandoned wagons. Reed's diary, the only first-hand source we have, as well as his subsequent reminiscences, agree that the Pioneer Palace was salvaged: on September 9, he wrote (using the curious third person in which his entire diary is written), "Mr Graves Mr Pike & Mr Brin loaned 2 Yoke of Cattle to J F Reed with one Yok[e] he had to bring his family wagon along." Later, he recalled that "there was no alternative but to leave everything but provisions, bedding and clothing. These were placed in the wagon that had been used for my family. I made a cache of everything else" (Korns 1951:214).

It was the beginning of the end for the Donner-Reed party. Seeing one's worldly goods simply abandoned to the elements had a psychological effect that one can only imagine, though its manifestations in terms of increased selfishness and bickering through the rest of the trip are well enough documented. Such animals as remained were exhausted beyond complete recovery, and the pace of the party, which needed to increase now that they had gained solid terrain, had to continue slowly. Some members of the party, in particular the Eddy family, were reduced to destitution, and few of the others still had an inclination to share their meager resources.

The remainder of the tragic story is too familiar to need retelling here except in summary (Stewart 1936; McGlashan 1880). Progress toward and along the Humboldt River was slow, and seething resentments flared up: Reed and Snyder fought, resulting in Snyder's death and Reed's banishment from the company; Breen and Eddy fought, in Eddy's extremity, over food and water; and old man Hardcoop fell behind and was left to die in the cold. When they reached the mountains, their daily progress, because of the emaciated and exhausted animals and people, could often be measured in feet as easily as in miles. At last, time ran out and the snow came, trapping them not far below the summit, where roughly half of them died of starvation, exposure, and perhaps even of murder by cannibalistic companions.

As one might expect, news of the Donner tragedy had a discouraging effect on wagon travel over the Hastings Cutoff (Kelly 1952a:3–30, Kelly 1952b:30–55). During the next two years, 1847 and 1848, no wagon parties used the route, and only three horseback parties are known to have crossed it, all eastbound travelers from California. Two of the parties used the route in 1847. The first, which left Sutter's Fort on June 2, consisted of the mountain man Miles Goodyear and several companions who brought a herd of horses to Utah. Curious about the reasons for the Donners' fate, they deliberately followed their back trail, but made no mention in the skimpy sources that exist for the trip of sighting abandoned equipment. The first such recorded sighting came from the second 1847 party, which was a sick detachment from the Mormon Battalion under Captain James Brown, who crossed the trail in the fall. Abner Blackburn, whose diary is our main source on the trip, recorded that while on the salt flats, they "Stopt at some abandoned wagons we weare cold pulled the wagons together set them an fire and had a good warm [camp?] tied the horses threw them the wood [food] to eat rolled up in our blankets and the first night on the desert was gone" (Kelly 1952a:7–8). Another party of Mormon Battalion returnees used the trail in 1848, but little is known of them.

It should not be surprising that the gold rush which began in 1849 and caused men to throw caution to the wind in so many other ways should also revive use of that reckless trail, the Hastings Cutoff. Even at that, most of those who reached California by the overland route in that year used the Salt Lake Cutoff to the north of the Great Salt Lake, which was becoming known as a better, if less direct, route. Though some are known to have used the Hastings Cutoff, there are no surviving diaries, and their experiences are known to us only through references in diaries of others who took the Salt Lake Cutoff and met them elsewhere on the trail. At that, no more than two or three groups probably chose the more direct crossing of the salt flats. Captain Howard Stansbury's survey party of that year accomplished the best documented crossing of the Hastings trail. An account of his experiences is contained in the following chapter.

The overland travel to California in 1850 dramatically exceeded even that of 1849, which had been by far the largest to date, and though most continued to use the Salt Lake Cutoff, others who thought they could steal a march on the rest of the mob spilled over onto the Hastings Cutoff. The term "Hastings Cutoff," incidentally, by 1850 meant only that part of the route to the south of the Great Salt Lake and across the salt flats. Travel over the eastern part of the old Hastings Cutoff had been greatly improved by development of Parley Pratt's "Golden Pass" road down the canyon that today bears his name, and by the widening of the Weber Canyon route for easy wagon travel, so that reaching Salt Lake City was no longer difficult. And reaching Salt Lake City had become largely a necessity in 1850, since the trail was so clogged with gold rushers that the small supply posts like Forts Laramie, Bridger, and Hall were simply swamped with customers. So the detour to Salt Lake City became a common practice.

Since most of the California-bound travelers of 1850 were prospectors rather than settlers, most used pack animals rather than wagons, and in spite of the fact that, in Charles Kelly's opinion, the trail during July and August saw an almost continuous stream of such parties, few experienced any extreme suffering. Those few parties who attempted to cross the desert with wagons, though, continued to find that the rigors of the crossing reduced them to fairly desperate circumstances before they reached water. The party of some three hundred gold seekers led by Auguste Archambeau, who had been a guide for Frémont and Stansbury, included pack animals but consisted mostly of ox-drawn wagons. When they reached Pilot Springs, they sent warnings back to Salt Lake City for those who might be tempted to follow, and in fact their party experienced the only recorded human death in the history of the Hastings Cutoff—a truly remarkable statistic, given the difficulty of the route and the numbers of people who crossed it.

Of those who crossed the desert that summer, the party of John Wood, which consisted of twenty-four men and ox-drawn wagons, is of special interest because Wood's journal records that they were forced by the difficulty of the crossing to abandon a wagon. "Notwithstanding it is heart-cheering to see water and grass," Wood wrote at Pilot Springs, "our team is broken and we must leave McLean's last wagon." Like the Bartleson-Bidwell emigrants, the Wood party made pack saddles from wagon parts and loaded their goods upon the oxen, "as many others have had to do" (Kelly 1952a:24).

Although overland emigration to California continued unabated through the 1850s, the gold rushers of 1850 were the last travelers of whom we have record who used the Hastings Cutoff. The suddenness of cessation of use of the route is interesting and not entirely explicable, though one suspects that travelers that year had sufficient opportunity to compare notes with those who had used the Salt Lake Cutoff, and learned that the southern route's supposed advantages were illusory. Virtually every journal of the Hastings Cutoff is replete with stories of suffering and delays to salvage wagons and recuperate animals, and it seems a reasonable assumption that the trail's bad reputation had become widely enough circulated that after 1850 no one any longer saw good reason to attempt it.

THREE

Howard Stansbury's Expedition to the Great Salt Lake, 1849–50*

Brigham D. Madsen

To expansionists in the United States of 1848, the capture of the great Southwest from Mexico appeared to be just the first salvo in the conquest of the entire western hemisphere. As one excited politician proclaimed, it was manifestly the destiny of the American eagle to fly over all the region from the Aurora Borealis on the north to Tierra del Fuego in the south. Of course, while plans matured for the next great territorial addition, something must be done to explore what had already been gained in the area stretching from the Rockies to the Pacific Coast and from the forty-second parallel to the Rio Grande.

The government agency assigned the task of scientific investigation of the Southwest and the Great Basin was the Corps of Topographical Engineers created out of the Army Reorganization Act of July 5, 1838. Under the skilled leadership of John J. Abert, the Corps had already sponsored the famous expeditions of John C. Frémont before the War with Mexico and had sent First Lieutenant William H. Emory as topographer with General Stephen W. Kearny's Army of the West to California (Emory 1848; Frémont 1843, 1845; Goetzmann 1959; Schubert 1980). With peace at hand, the Corps now looked forward to intensive exploration of the newly acquired region, and among the first targets was to be an examination of the Great Salt Lake and the recent Mormon settlements which formed a way station for the

---

*Part of this chapter appeared in the *Utah Historical Quarterly* 56, no. 2 (Spring 1988) 148–59.

thousands of gold-hungry emigrants on their way to the new diggings in California.

Colonel Abert outlined the objectives of the 1849 expedition to experienced Captain Howard Stansbury whom he chose to head the survey party along with an assistant, First Lieutenant John Williams Gunnison. The captain was instructed to observe and "confirm" the well-traveled Oregon Trail from Fort Leavenworth to Fort Hall; to explore a wagon route from the latter place to the north end of Great Salt Lake; to determine facilities for a "landing place" on the lake for the shipment of supplies from the Mormon settlements to Fort Hall; to survey the Great Salt Lake and determine its capacity for navigation; to survey the Jordan River and Utah Lake; to evaluate the ability of the Mormon settlers to provide food and other supplies for Fort Hall and overland travelers and to report on the population, mills, work force, and Indians in the region; to make their home in "Mormon City" and to employ Mormons on a temporary basis during the survey; and finally to locate a site for a military post in the Great Salt Lake area (Abert 1849). There may also have been a hidden agenda understood by Abert and Stansbury that the captain was also to discreetly determine the loyalty of the Mormons and their present attitude toward the government of the United States now that they were again under American jurisdiction.

To accomplish these various ends would require a leader of rare diplomatic skill and genial disposition, one who could win the confidence of Brigham Young and the Mormon people and yet who could make a cold-eyed and impartial appraisal of the situation in Salt Lake City. Colonel Abert also needed a commander who was not too gung ho as a military man, but who could ingratiate himself to get the aid necessary for the accomplishment of his objectives. An individual of broad interests and humanitarian in point of view would aid this cause. And if the man were a good observer and with literary qualifications able to describe clearly and succinctly what he saw, so much better. Howard Stansbury seemed to fit the bill as one of the few non-West Pointers who had spent a number of years outside the military as a civil engineer. Later on, both Gunnison and Mormon Albert Carrington would complain that Stansbury was too relaxed and informal in his approach to his army duties, although both would concede the captain was always thoroughly in command of the expedition. Howard Stansbury was just a civilian engineer first and a military man second (Anonymous 1888, 1975; Malone 1935).

Lieutenant Gunnison, a graduate of West Point, also had extensive experience with the Topographical Engineers, having joined the Corps in 1838. He spent most of the decade before this Salt Lake trip as a surveyor with parties engaged in work in the Great Lakes region where he spent long hours in the field in the summers and in agency offices in the winters "drawing maps of our survey through the day, and in our parlors sociably at night" (Booth 1860; Gunnison 1843; Mumey 1955). Gunnison was more introspective than Stansbury, but was energetic and decisive as an engineer and was a man of deep religious views. He was to have the opportunity of observing the unique religion of the Utah Saints and of describing them in his book, *The Mormons*. Together with Stansbury's official *Report*, the two works would inform the nation and the world about the geographic features of the Great Salt Lake area and the theological beliefs and cultural qualities of the Mormon people (Stansbury 1852a; Gunnison 1852).

Most of the records of the Stansbury Expedition are located in two boxes in the U.S. National Archives. These leather-bound report books consist of twelve journals—six volumes by Stansbury, four by Gunnison, one by Albert Carrington, and one by John Hudson. Carrington, who became the straw boss of the survey crew and accompanied Stansbury back to Washington, D.C., to help prepare the *Report*, was a college-trained scientist and prominent Mormon leader who at the time was serving as Brigham Young's secretary (Heath n.d.). John Hudson was a well-educated young Englishman and artist who was forced by ill health to stop off in Salt Lake City in the fall of 1849 on his way to the goldfields (Figure 4). Stansbury hired him as an artist to draw sketches of scenes around Great Salt Lake, many of which appear in the finished *Report* (Madsen 1981). Hudson's and Stansbury's journals are real literary productions, exhibiting skills in writing and interesting observations and descriptions of the geography and flora and fauna encountered. Gunnison and Carrington have left us rather prosaic and pragmatic accounts of meteorological and technical accomplishments. There are also two private journals left by Carrington—a small notebook held by the University of Utah concerned with the survey of Utah Lake and a second larger diary of his trip to Washington, D.C., and the winter of 1851 spent there. It is in the possession of the Daughters of Utah Pioneers in Salt Lake City. Finally, there are sixteen field notebooks in the National Archives boxes concerned chiefly with engineering data and a number of rough sketches which were no doubt helpful in preparing the two maps produced by the

CAVE ON FREMONT'S ISLAND.

Figure 4. Typical view of Stansbury expedition camp produced by expedition artist John Hudson (from Madsen 1989; original in Stansbury [1852a]).

expedition and in fleshing out some details of the survey but of minimum interest to historians or general readers today.

Although the Stansbury group was to leave Fort Leavenworth in company with a regiment of Mounted Rifles destined for Fort Hall and Oregon, the captain was late in reaching Leavenworth and so eventually started along the Oregon Trail with only his crew of French Canadians and a small party of California-bound emigrants under Mr. and Mrs. Charles C. Sackett. They left at the end of May 1849 with eighteen men in the Stansbury Expedition and six people in the Sackett caravan. Lieutenant Gunnison was so ill at the beginning of the journey that he was confined to an army ambulance and spent most of the trip inside the vehicle with the leather blinds drawn and his only solace some long letters which he wrote to his wife describing the hardships of travel (Madsen 1989). Stansbury seemed to enjoy the excursion across the plains and has left a very descriptive and interesting account of the gold rush of that year – the overburdened emigrants, the deaths from cholera, and the sights and sounds of traveling through Indian country (Stansbury 1852a; Madsen 1989).

At Fort Bridger, Gunnison was sufficiently recovered from his illness to take command of the main party and lead it into Salt Lake City while Stansbury with guide Jim Bridger and a "couple of men" left to reconnoiter a shorter route from Fort Bridger to the north end of Great Salt Lake. After wandering around in this craggy portion of the Wasatch Range, the captain and a no doubt bemused Jim Bridger finally descended through North Ogden Canyon to come out into the Salt Lake Valley at Brown's Settlement where Stansbury recorded:

> Upon requesting food and lodging for the night, we were told to our great surprise that we could not be accommodated, nor would the occupants sell us so much as an egg or a cup of milk, so that we were obliged to remount our horses; and we actually bivouacked under some willows, within a hundred yards of this inhospitable dwelling . . . of this surly Nabal (Stansbury 1852a:83–84).

After this inauspicious introduction to Mormon hospitality, Stansbury rode into the city of the Saints with some apprehension about how he might be received by the chief Mormon, Brigham Young.

Gunnison had already met suspicion from the Mormon leader and wrote of his first meeting with Young and Albert Carrington: "We had a few moments' talk about our 'Survey.' . . . Under most apparent indifference he showed anxiety — & I hear from various sources that our survey is regarded with great jealousy—and have had warning that secret means would be used to prevent any maps being made of the valley even that our lives are in danger, as a hint from *the one man* could take them" (Madsen 1989). Thus warned, Stansbury determined to meet at once with Brigham Young and learned that around the Mormon people, "The impression was that a survey was to be made of their country in the same manner that other public lands are surveyed, for the purpose of dividing it into townships and sections, and of thus establishing and recording the claims of the Government to it, and thereby anticipating any claim the Mormons might set up from their previous occupation." Using all of his skills of diplomacy and persuasion, Stansbury was finally able to undeceive Young "to his entire satisfaction" and clinched the agreement by hiring the Mormon president's private secretary, Albert Carrington, as a chief assistant to the survey (Stansbury 1852a). As Young explained in a private letter, this "will enable us to know at all times what their movements & discoveries are. Capt Stansbury's expressed feelings & appearance are very friendly" (Young 1849).

With good relationships established in the Mormon community and leaving Gunnison and Carrington to spend the autumn in surveying the Jordan River and Utah Valley, Stansbury now embarked on a reconnaissance of a practical wagon road from Salt Lake City to Fort Hall and a preliminary exploration of the northern shores of Great Salt Lake and the salt desert extending west from the lake to Pilot Peak. With John Owen, the sutler for the Mounted Rifles, and his geologist-scientist, Dr. James Blake, the captain left Salt Lake City on September 12, 1849; explored "an excellent wagon road" to Fort Hall; returned with the supplies expected from Fort Leavenworth; made a reconnaissance of Cache Valley as a wintering site for his government stock; and then started around Great Salt Lake and across the salt flats (Stansbury 1852a; Madsen 1989).

Stansbury's purpose was to gain some knowledge of its general features, but he was warned "By the old mountain-men [that] such a reconnaissance was considered not only hazardous in the highest degree, but absolutely impracticable, especially so late a season of the year" (Stansbury 1852a). Undismayed, Stansbury and his party left Bear River on October 20 guided by the French-Canadian Archambeau, who had traversed the salt desert with John C. Frémont in 1845. After much hardship during which his mules were "deprived of almost all sustenance for more than sixty hours," the exploring party reached one of a series of springs at the base of Pilot Peak. After camping for four nights at the springs, Stansbury and his party headed east retracing the trail followed by Frémont, Hastings, and the Donner-Reed party. Stansbury's journal entries for the following two days are cited at length:

Friday Nov 2

Ther. Sunrise 19– Packed up & started on our journey. There lies before us 70 miles without water or grass. Packed 18 gall Keg & our India rubb[e]r bags together with as much grass as the mules could carry. We have to recross the bay crossed on Monday but more to the South at the S end of the large Butte where we slept Sunday night. The course from camp is East, but we followed the edge of the bay South 2-1/2 miles to a point where a road from Mormon City crosses to take advantage of the beaten track as the mud is quite soft. At this point there are several excellent large springs & a numerous company of emigrants have lately encamped there [these are probably those currently listed as Donner Springs on USGS maps]. The road runs around the foot of the Ridge, passes to the north of another high one (crossed by Fremont) & then goes on to the head of Marys River [now known as the Humboldt]. It is evident that the whole of Sundays travel and perhaps a part of Saturdays has been too far to the West, as we have left the lake entirely But it was impossible to proceed to the South on account of the miry nature of the mud sand & the almost certainty of finding no water. Leaving the springs last mentioned we followed the road (which is called Hastings Cut off) across the mud plain which was now quite moist from recent showers, a distance of about 9 miles, when we rose a gentle neck of land connecting the South ridge upon which we encamped on Sunday night with another to the south of it which runs considerably to the S. W. [probably the Bonneville Lake beach feature between the Silver Island Range and Crater Island presently known as Donner-Reed Pass]. Here we stopped to give the mules a last chance for a little bunch grass which grew in scattered patches on the mountain to the South ⌒⌒⌒⌒ E by S. before us for a the point where we will have to cross a high ridge or mountain distant 40 or 45 miles & which from present appearances must form the S W boundary of the Lake. Between us & it is a low flat mud plain, a continuation of that crossed on Sunday night ~~The~~ A long high ridge or mountain rises out of the plain before us about 20 miles long & as many distant, the Northern end of which we left on sunday night [probably here Stansbury refers to the Newfoundland Mountains]. It bears N E by N. The S end bears E by N.

The route we are now taking was first followed by Fremont in 1845, from Mormon City. A year afterward by an Emigrant party under a Mr Hastings, whence its name.

Change of color of salt plains

After halting an hour we pursued our course along the eastern base of the southern butte for 3 or 4 miles. It consists of altered black limestone seamed with veins of gypsum all altered by fire. Two miles farther on is an isolated butte [probably Floating Island] pushed up thro the plain. From this we travelled on until midnight lighted by the moon which struggled thro a mass of dark clouds threatening rain. The wind was fresh from the South, & the level plain over which we passed was soft and sticky mud moistened by the last rain which made the travelling very laborious heavy & slow. We passed during the night 4 wagons and one cart, with innumerable articles of clothing, tools chests trunks books & yokes, chains, & some half dozen dead oxen. Encamped on the wet sand & had for wood part of an ox yoke & the remains of a barrel & part of an old wagon bed. The whole plain is as desolate barren & dreary as can well be imagined. Gave the mules some grass which we had packed on them in the morning & two pint cups of water each & tied them to keep them from wandering off Night windy & cold

Saturday Nov 3

Off half hour ~~befo~~ after sunrise. The wind blew very hard over the level plain & altho the there[r] was only 47° yet it was intensely cold. Great coats leggings & all appliances were put in req[n] to keep in the animal heat. Continued on the same general course following the emigrant road which however is quite crooked. The road is very muddy & sticky making travelling very laborious. There being no wood for cooking, we started without breakfasting, & travelled until noon a distance of 10 or 12 miles, when crossing a ridge running N & W [probably the Grayback Hills] We sheltered ourselves behind it in the hollow, built a fire & ~~coo~~ boiled our coffee, which with cold bread & meat (bacon) formed the only meal we had during the whole day. Two of the mules gave out before reaching this point, but they were with great trouble driven up. The mules having been without water since yesterday morn[g] except what little was served out to them last night after filling our canteens, the remainder of our small stock was divided among them & we continued our journey toward the mountain which lay some dozen miles before us. I had intended to cross it today but it was dark before the pack reached the Northern ["Western" written above this word] slope [this is probably the Cedar Mountains], where we encamped amongst plenty of cedar & large sage, which was very welcome to us, as the day had been blustering all day, & there was every prospect of a heavy rain, whilst it was quite cold & raw. Large fires from dry cedar & sage were soon blazing & every one was tired enough to seek his blanket without going to the trouble of preparing the evening meal. The two mules which had given out during the morning gave out again in the afternoon & had to be left behind. We are encamped at the eastern base of the mountain where the road crosses it through a long & winding pass. Night dark & blustering with rain.

Stansbury reached Salt Lake City on November 7, 1849, "being the first party of white men that ever succeeded in making the entire circuit of the lake by land" (Stansbury 1852a; Madsen 1989). With cold weather ending their survey of Utah Lake, Gunnison now joined Stansbury in Salt Lake City for the winter season where the two men had a lengthy opportunity of observing the culture and life-style of their Mormon hosts. Unlike passing emigrants and short-term visitors who too often pronounced anathema upon the religious and marital practices of the Mormons, the two army officers enjoyed friendly communication which resulted in a far more understanding attitude and sympathy for their beleaguered neighbors than the world generally accorded them.

The only incident to mar a rather peaceful winter of writing up notes and preparing for the survey of Great Salt Lake in the spring was an Indian battle at Fort Utah (now Provo) at Utah Lake (Madsen 1981; Christy 1978). By April 4, 1850, Stansbury and Gunnison were ready to begin the main project of their assignment, the survey of Great Salt Lake. Gunnison and his men were to examine and measure the settled east and south shores of the lake while Stansbury, Carrington, and Hudson were to tackle the more difficult task of chaining the forbidding northern and western shorelines. Gunnison had the easier mission because he and his group had access to the farms along the east side and a convenient base of supplies at Salt Lake City. Stansbury and Carrington, on the other hand, were always running out of drinking water and the beef which they learned to salt down with lake water, had to endure the interminable attacks of midges and mosquitoes, and were engaged in a constant fight to keep their two boats afloat when the winds would drive them off the water, leaving them stuck on the mud flats. The three-month effort included a near mutiny when the cook quit, a night of sailing in bitter cold and stormy weather which almost resulted in Stansbury's death, and a few balmy and pleasant days when the captain and Hudson could revel in the delight of bathing in the salty water or in observing the antics of the numerous pelicans on the various islands. It was a real adventure story capped by a successful survey of the lake and its environs (Madsen 1981, 1989).

Satisfied with the completion of their surveys of the Salt Lake, Jordan River, and Utah Lake, Stansbury and Gunnison then spent July and part of August in the process of triangulation of the three areas so as to gain the engineering data needed for the first accurate map of the entire region (Madsen 1981, 1989). The process was interrupted on July 24, 1850, by attendance at the annual Pioneer Day celebration where, as distinguished guests, the two army officers were called to deliver toasts at the formal banquet and to hear one read in their honor. Stansbury displayed his customary sensitivity by declaring, "Freedom of thought; freedom of speech; freedom of the Press; and the more inestimable freedom to worship our God just as we please." Not to be outdone, Mormon Patriarch John Smith reciprocated with words of praise for the army engineers. "Capt. Stansbury, and the officers under his command, are worthy of praise for their prudence, perseverance, industry, benevolence and urbanity: they have done their work honorably for their country; may honor, fame and power be their portion forever" (Anonymous 1850).

With such friendly encomiums ringing in their ears, the government surveyors left the city of the Saints on August 28, 1850, bound for the East and the families from whom they had been parted for over a year. Instead of backtracking via the Oregon Trial, Stansbury decided to reconnoiter a new and more direct route across Wyoming from Fort Bridger due east to a connection with the well-rutted Oregon road at Fort Laramie. His course was destined to become the route followed by the Pony Express and, later, the Union Pacific Railroad, so it has some significance for the history of the American West. Before reaching Laramie, Stansbury suffered an injury to his leg on October 6 which forced him to ride in an army ambulance for the rest of the trip. He allowed the myth to be perpetuated that he had suffered a fall from his horse, but Carrington reported the real reason in his personal diary: "even Capt$^{\underline{n}}$ hurt himself kicking one of his dogs out of his tent." From this point on, Stansbury ceased making entries in his journal, and we must rely on Gunnison and Carrington for details of the rest of the return trip (Carrington 1850–51; Madsen 1989).

At Fort Laramie, the expedition split up with Stansbury and Gunnison going on ahead, while Carrington was detailed to wait at the post for the expedition records and equipment which a Mormon leader, Orson Hyde, was bringing on from Salt Lake City. Picking up this baggage, Carrington transported it to Fort Leavenworth and then traveled on to Washington, D.C., which he reached on December 13, 1850, prepared to spend the next four months aiding Stansbury and Gunnison in preparing the two maps and the other records for the formal *Report* of the surveys (Carrington 1850–51). Meanwhile, the captain and lieutenant had departed for home to spend some leave with their families before reporting to the nation's capital (Madsen 1989).

There are no extant journals by Stansbury and Gunnison describing the winter's work in Washington, and except for a few letters by Gunnison to his wife, we are left to depend on a personal diary kept by Carrington for details of the daily routine at Stansbury's office (Carrington 1850–51). Carrington has left an interesting account not only of the official work of the survey team but also of life in the capital as he met important political figures and indulged in the kind of sight-seeing typical of first-time visitors to the city on the Potomac.

Carrington left for his home in Salt Lake City on May 9, 1851, and our journal accounts of the Stansbury Expedition end with this entry.

The Stansbury *Report* was published in 1852 as a congressional document and also in a private printing by the Lippincott, Grambo & Company of Philadelphia. While the *Report* was widely read at the time, Captain Howard Stansbury's expedition to the Great Salt Lake has for too long been relegated to a short note in the history of the American West. Overshadowed by such flamboyant explorers as John C. Frémont and lacking the ability or motivation to dramatize himself and his exploits like a J. W. Powell, Stansbury's significant accomplishments have not received the attention they deserve. His interesting and descriptive portrayal of the great California Gold Rush of 1849 across the plains ranks with that of J. Goldsborough Bruff and other well-known accounts. He and Dr. James Blake were among the first to postulate that the terraces they observed along the mountainsides ringing the Great Salt Lake were evidences of a large prehistoric lake in the Great Basin. In his exploration of the sea of salt, he gave the country its first accurate map of the area as well as leaving his name to the largest island in the lake and the range of mountains just beyond and attaching Gunnison's and Carrington's names to two other large islands. He reconnoitered a new road between Salt Lake City and Fort Hall that later became part of the Montana Trail and established the feasibility of the route through southern Wyoming which was to become the Union Pacific access through the Continental Divide. And in the process of almost two years of such exploration, he maintained command of his expedition and did not lose a man to accident or disease.

Aided by a competent assistant, Lieutenant Gunnison, and by a conscientious surveyor-foreman in the person of Albert Carrington, Stansbury took back to Washington, D.C., and the reading public of the East and Europe an important description of the Great Salt Lake and the Great Basin and of the Mormon settlers who now occupied this northern section of the new Mexican Cession. The widespread acceptance of his publication was aided in no small measure by the fact that the narrative and descriptive passages in the document and in Stansbury's personal journals are superb literature. The journals, correspondence, and other documents of the Stansbury Expedition provide a significant and striking record of the events of 1849 and 1850 along the Oregon Trail and in the Valley of Great Salt Lake (Madsen 1989).

FOUR

Previous Expeditions to the Abandoned Wagon Sites

*H*oward Stansbury and his party were by no means the only visitors to disturb the Donner-Reed party wagons. Fourteen other recorded expeditions preceded the 1986 excavations at the suspected wagon sites, and there were doubtless innumerable other unrecorded visits that resulted in some degree of destruction to the wagons and their contents. The sites were initially disturbed by a detachment of Mormon Battalion soldiers in 1847, and again in 1849 by Stansbury's explorers. The sites were rediscovered during the 1870s by cattlemen who observed that some of the wagons were still standing. The wagons had collapsed by 1897 but surface remains continued to be visible well into the 1930s. By 1957, little remained to suggest that wagons once stood at the sites.

1870s EXPEDITION

Cattlemen Dan Hunt, Quince Knowlton, and Steven S. Worthington of Grantsville, Utah, discovered the remains of wagons "deserted in the deep mud" while herding cattle across the salt flats about 1875. After examining the remains, they observed that "some had fallen down and had begun to collect mounds of sand." Fragments of the canvas wagon covers still clung to the bows. Many of the wheels were still fairly well preserved (Kelly 1930).

1897 EXPEDITION

Steven S. Worthington and Quince Knowlton returned to the sites on June 18, 1897, with Hamp Worthington, Saul Worthington, and a

Mr. Vanderhoff to bring in the wagons and associated artifacts for the Jubilee Parade of 1897. After arriving at the site with a wagon and saddle horse, the expedition members noted that none of the wagons were still standing. The expedition removed ox bones, ox yokes, ox shoes, a log chain, and a medicine chest containing bottles of rosin, turpentine, and camphor from the site, loaded them into the wagon, and returned to Grantsville. Upon return, the expedition members turned the material over to the president of the committee for the Jubilee of 1897. Subsequent disposition of the artifacts by the committee is unknown (Worthington to Kelly 1930).

1927 EXPEDITION

Charles E. Davis of Los Angeles visited the wagon sites in 1927. Davis removed artifacts from the sites and returned with them to California where they were exhibited for a time at the California State Capitol and Sutter's Fort Museum in Sacramento. Some of the specimens are currently on exhibit at Donner Memorial State Park, Truckee, California. Details of the expedition and recovered artifacts have not been located. Mike Tucker, curator of Sutter's Fort State Historic Site, indicates that the remaining Davis items might be stored in the museum annex. The current collections management project, however, has not yet progressed to the point where they can be easily located or identified.

1929 EXPEDITIONS

Four expeditions set out to explore the wagon sites in 1929. The first expedition party included Charles Kelly of Salt Lake City, Dan Orr of Skull Valley, and Frank Durfee of Grantsville, Utah. The group embarked from Orr's Skull Valley ranch in Kelly's Model A Ford following the trail left by emigrants traveling the Hastings Cutoff route to California. Traveling north and west, the expedition encountered five sites on Grayback Ridge and in the sand dunes west of the ridge before entering the salt flats. The sites included scatters of surface artifacts and charcoal concentrations suggesting that parties of emigrants camped here or lightened their loads before entering the flats. Artifacts observed or collected from the sites included: tinware vessels, broken bottles, wood fragments, broken jugs, two Kentucky-style rifles, a cobbler's hammer, a bitters bottle, wooden bucket staves, square nails, pots and pan lids, jug stoppers, a barrel bung, tent stakes, a chestnut board marked "H.R.," wagon timbers, ox yokes, and an "old army canteen of the period 1845."

Once on the flats, the expedition observed two sites before becoming mired in the mud and having to turn back. The first site was located at the "Birds Nests," a group of rough-legged hawks nests located approximately 11 miles northwest of the dunes. The site consisted of a charcoal concentration, wagon parts, running gear, and an artifact scatter which included a broken blue china saucer, a white china plate fragment, rope, leather boot soles containing wooden pegs, and the remains of a tar bucket.

The second site, photographed by Kelly (Figure 5), was located northwest of the "birds nests." The position of landmarks in the photograph suggest that this site is the site designated 42To468 during the 1986 expedition (compare Figures 5 and 6). The 1929 photograph shows a wagon axle and bolster partially covered by a low sand dune. The expedition also discovered an empty wagon box at the site covered by the dune. Kelly dismantled the wagon box, removing planks from the site to free his car which had become mired in mud near the site. After freeing their vehicle, the expedition members returned to Skull Valley. Artifacts collected during the expedition were donated to Grantsville High School and the "Salt Lake City Historical Museum." The artifact collection from Grantsville High School has been transferred to the Donner-Reed Memorial Museum in Grantsville, where it is presently located. The R. L. Polk Salt Lake City Directories fail to list a "Salt Lake City Historical Museum." Only two museums, LDS Museum and the University of Utah museum, are listed prior to 1934. Records from both museums fail to list any donations from Charles Kelly or any other of the expedition members.

Later in 1929, three expeditions headed northwest from Wendover, Utah, following the Silver Island Mountains to the pass separating the Silver Island Range from the Crater Island Range. Expedition members included Charles and Dwight Kelly of Salt Lake City, Dan Orr of Skull Valley, Frank Durfee of Grantsville, and Edgar Ledyard. Leaving their vehicle at the pass, the expedition members followed the Hastings road east onto the salt flats. Just north of Floating Island, they discovered a barrelhead (Figure 7), barrel staves, hickory barrel hoops, a flintlock rifle barrel, and a folding brass comb. The barrelhead is in the collection of the Donner-Reed Memorial Museum.

Figure 5. 1929 photograph of a site thought to be 42To468. View is west toward Floating Island and Silver Island. Note wagon axle and bolster eroding out of the dune. Photo credit: Utah State Historical Society.

Figure 6. 1986 photograph looking west from site 42To468 toward Floating Island and Silver Island.

Figure 7. Photograph from the 1929 expedition of Dwight Kelly examining a barrelhead north of Floating Island. The barrelhead is part of the collection at the Donner-Reed Memorial Museum, Grantsville, Utah. Photo credit: Utah State Historical Society.

Two or three miles east the expeditions encountered the first of three low sand dunes which contained buried ox skeletons and wagon parts. The first site consisted of a long low dune which had covered four associated wagon wheels. Only the hubs were exposed (Figure 8). One hub contained the broken end of an axle. Expedition members excavated part of the site with bare hands and recovered the remains of logging chains and wood fragments from planks and axles. Location, description, and excavation activity at this site suggest that it is the same site designated 42To470 by the 1986 expedition.

The second dune was located east of the first and was smaller in size. This site contained iron, a few boards, and an ox skeleton. This site may be that designated 42To471 by the 1986 expedition.

The third dune was located east of the second and west of the site where Kelly's car became mired. The site was described as consisting of "two heaps representing wagons" (Figure 9). Ox bones were observed between the "heaps." Location and description of this site suggest that it is the site designated 42To469 by the 1986 expedition.

Figure 8. Photograph from the 1929 expedition of a wagon site east of Floating Island. Note wagon wheel hubs partially covered by the dune. Photo credit: Utah State Historical Society.

Figure 9. Photograph from the 1929 expedition of a wagon site thought to be 42To469. View is west with Floating Island and Silver Island in the background. Photo credit: Utah State Historical Society.

The expeditions failed to find a complete wagon or any small items such as dishes, bottles, or tools at any of the wagon sites. Nothing remained but heavy pieces of iron, log chains, and scattered fragments of wood. Artifacts collected during the expedition were donated to Grantsville High School (Kelly 1930).

1930 EXPEDITIONS

Two expeditions led by Frank Durfee and Dan Orr set out to visit the wagon sites in 1930. Frank Durfee and a group of Grantsville High School students located the site of an abandoned wagon box approximately 1/2 mile north of the "Birds Nests." The expedition described the site as consisting of a low sand dune which covered the wagon box and an ox yoke. The wagon box contained a cast-iron stove, broken dishes, tools, chain, bottles, a feather bed, and remnants of books. No running gear or wheels were associated with the site. The artifacts were collected and donated to Grantsville High School.

Dan Orr collected wagon wheels, log chains, wagon tires, water jugs, and tools from an unspecified location "on high ground above the salt flats." These items were donated to Grantsville High School.

1936 EXPEDITION

Walter M. Stookey and Nephi L. Morris of Salt Lake City, Raleigh Johnson, a Mr. Pettit of Grantsville, and an unidentified passenger formed the expedition party of 1936. They set out from Knolls, Utah, in September to explore the Hastings Cutoff trail and abandoned wagon sites. The expedition utilized a converted caterpillar tractor and covered trailer to cross the salt flats (Figure 10).

The expedition's expressed intentions were to record the trail with "pictures and written description." Few of the expedition's written descriptions or observations have been located. Observations are limited to the following remarks from Walter Stookey's book *Fatal Decision:* "We had not advanced more than a mile into this part of the desert [the eastern edge of the salt flats] before we began to discover abandoned materials that had been left behind. These consisted mainly of fragments of wagons and various pieces of household furniture all in rather advanced stages of decay or disintegration."

About a mile further on, the expedition arrived at a location which Stookey interpreted as the site of James Reed's abandoned wagons. He states that from this site, "we recovered sufficient parts to reconstruct roughly one rear wheel." Additional notes, referred to by

Figure 10. Photograph from the 1936 expedition of the caterpillar tractor and trailer used for transportation across the mud flats. Photo credit: Utah State Historical Society.

Stookey, which may have described and identified the location of his discoveries have never been located. According to a conversation with Corrine Dods, a relative from Salt Lake City, it appears as though they may have been disposed of shortly after Stookey's death in 1951.

The expedition photographs taken by Nephi L. Morris contain few recognizable landmarks. They show a site designated "Cemetery of the Desert" (Figures 11 and 12). A lack of identifiable landmarks makes it impossible to identify one precise location of this site.

The photographs of the site show two wide planks with nail stains at each end partially covered by a sand dune. The planks, a five-foot diameter wagon wheel, an iron tire, and numerous other items are shown stacked on a table (Figure 13) at the University of Utah Museum sometime in the 1930s or 40s. Current efforts to relocate these items have been unsuccessful.

1956 EXPEDITION

In August 1956, two jeeps carrying Henry J. Webb, David E. Miller, C. Gregory Crampton, Kenneth Eble, Steven R. Hailes, Wendell Taylor, Wes Taylor, and David H. Miller set off from Knolls, Utah, in an effort to trace the precise routes used by emigrants on the Hastings Cutoff to cross the Great Salt Lake Desert. Like Kelly in 1929, the expedition's vehicles became mired in the mud before reaching the

Figure 11. 1936 expedition photograph of a site designated as "Cemetery of the Desert."

Figure 12. Closeup view of the "Cemetery of the Desert."

wagon sites and had to turn back. The expedition drove to Pilot Springs and attempted to follow the route from west to east. The jeeps again became mired east of Floating Island before reaching the site of the wagons (Webb 1956, 1957).

1957 EXPEDITION

On August 10, 1957, Henry J. Webb and Gerard Cantero successfully followed the Hastings Cutoff route in a jeep from Knolls, Utah, to Pilot Springs, Nevada. They observed that "jettisoned articles no longer

Figure 13. Walter Stookey and former University of Utah President George Thomas at the University of Utah Museum, with artifacts collected during the 1936 expedition.

littered the route" as they had in the 1930s. At the site of the abandoned wagons, they observed that "two low mounds stand a hundred yards or less apart and in them and on them are bleached bone like pieces of wood and a few encrusted lengths of iron." Nothing else remained (Webb 1958, Miller 1958).

1962 EXPEDITION

An expedition including Henry J. Webb, Angus M. Woodbury, W. Claudell Johnson, and J. Derle Thorpe crossed the salt flats on August 17, 1962, in an effort to map the emigrant routes identified by Webb and Cantero in 1957. The expedition utilized three Trackmasters and one Spryte (tracked vehicles) for the crossing. The expedition noted that "four low mounds still exist" marking the location where the abandoned wagons once stood. Two of the mounds were excavated by expedition members (Figure 14). Recovered artifacts included a small

Figure 14. A wagon site being "excavated" by members of the 1962 expedition (from Webb [1963], reprinted with the permission of the Utah State Historical Society).

silver spoon, a compass, a locket, harness parts, ox yokes, a bottle, and wagon parts. Sand- and salt-encrusted pieces of metal, wood, and leather were observed "in and on" the mounds (Webb 1963, Fairbanks 1962).

In sum, information from the 15 recorded expeditions to the wagon sites indicates a gradual but continuous decay in the remains left by the Donner-Reed party. Most of this decay can be attributed to cultural rather than natural causes. The wagons appear to have been left in place for the most part, with their contents essentially intact. The wagons were initially disturbed, principally for fuel, by travelers actually using the Hastings Cutoff trail. Within 30 years, the wagons had begun to fall down and dunes were beginning to form around them. Within 50 years, all the wagons were down and most of their contents and many major wagon parts had been removed. By the centennial of the Donner-Reed trek, virtually all visible wagon parts and all but the smallest artifacts had been removed and what little remained was buried under a veneer of sand. Additional expeditions during the next 40 years removed many of the few remaining smaller objects, such as spoons and lockets, and by the fall of 1986 there seemed to be little of the wagons beyond small wood splinters and stains from oxidized iron.

Excavation Procedures

IDENTIFICATION OF THE WAGON SITES
The many previous expeditions to the wagon sites produced enough information, in the form of both documentary evidence and folklore, to generate widespread concern that valuable information and materials remained at the sites and that a pumping project might well destroy the last evidence of the Donner-Reed party's struggle. This concern led to an Air Force survey project, on a portion of the Hill Air Force Base north bombing range, designed to locate historical sites prior to flooding of the area. The project was led by John Grossnickle, Hill Air Force Base engineering technician/surveyor, and was intended to identify historical sites and materials referred to in Department of Interior Cadastral Survey field notes and plot their locations on a base map. The notes mention the "Remains of an ox team caravan, consisting of four wagons and bones of oxen" in T2N, R15W, Section 22. Based on this information, the Air Force team was eventually able to rediscover and identify five suspected wagon sites.

On July 22, 1986, Grossnickle, accompanied by Richard Fike, Dean Zeller, and Jack Peterson of the U.S. Bureau of Land Management, conducted a visual reconnaissance of the area with all-terrain vehicles. Starting from the boundary between Sections 21 and 22, the group drove east and west in random transects during which they discovered the site designated 42To470. This site consisted of a low mound containing fragments of rusted metal, wood, and bone. After locating 42To470, the group spread out and headed west to the pass separating the Silver Island Range from the Crater Island Range. No additional sites were located. From the pass, the group made a final wide sweep to the east and once again failed to find any additional sites.

Between September 11 and September 15, 1986, Grossnickle and his Hill Air Force Base survey crew composed of Jeff Sanders, Shane Gramling, and George Hart reexamined the area. Starting from site 42To470, the group began following two parallel discolored bands in the soil believed to be filled-in wagon wheel ruts from the Hastings Cutoff road. The group examined a corridor 200 yards from each side of the discolored area. One isolated rust stain and three additional sites (42To467–469) were located in Sections 22 and 26. These sites were marked and mapped. An additional site (42To471) was located and recorded during the mapping process (J. Grossnickle 1987 personal communication).

Transportation and Logistics

The five sites were located on the isolated mud flats of the Great Salt Lake Desert approximately 120 miles west of Salt Lake City and 35 miles northeast of Wendover, Utah/Nevada. The weather, isolated nature of the site locations, and the consistency of the mud flats upon which they are located created special transportation and logistical problems. Access required a daily three-hour round-trip drive via a four-wheel-drive vehicle from housing facilities at Wendover, Utah, or a base camp in the Silver Island Mountains. At Floating Island, an isolated eastern extension of the Silver Island range, the road abruptly comes to an end and the remaining three to five miles to the sites must be traveled cross-country. Travel by conventional vehicles across the semisolid mud flats is not advised, even in dry weather, due to their weight. The rusting hulks of 20-year-old vehicles rising out of the mud like monoliths serve as grim reminders of those who failed to heed such advice. Wet weather can make this transportation problem especially severe in the early winter since an afternoon thunderstorm can transform the mud flats into a series of shallow lakes in a matter of hours.

The lack of conventional transport made it difficult to ferry personnel and equipment to the sites and even more difficult to return with the excavated artifacts and/or the excavated mud containing the artifacts. Such material could not be water screened at the site because the nearest water source was five miles away. Preexcavation planning estimated the amount of mud or back dirt that would need to be transported to a water-screening station at approximately 450 cubic feet or 22,000 pounds of material! Fortunately field methods were employed that negated the need to transport dirt for screening. As a result, open all-terrain vehicles (Figure 15) and a utility trailer were used to transport personnel and equipment to the sites. As a backup, however, Utah National Guard helicopters stood by one day per week to aid in the transport of excavated back dirt in the event that the field methods employed failed to work, and U.S. Air Force Trackmasters were available on an emergency basis.

Because of the 120-mile distance to the division laboratories in Salt Lake City, an interim facility was sought for the temporary storage of artifacts and equipment. The crew at the Department of Transportation Maintenance Station 221 in Wendover, Utah, generously shared their facilities for this purpose.

FIELD METHODS

The five sites identified during the reconnaissance were initially marked with orange wooden lath posts which subsequently served as site datums. These datums were surveyed by Hill Air Force Base personnel and their locations plotted on the USGS 7.5-minute Floating Island NE Quadrangle map. Horizontal distance was recorded using an HP 3800 distance meter. Angles were recorded with a Carl Zeiss TH2 one second Theodolite. Topographic maps were made of the untested sites. Notes were made and photographs were taken prior to excavation. An MK22 metal detector was used to conduct a metal-detector reconnaissance of each site. Concentrations of metal were marked with pin flags and mapped.

Following the initial reconnaissance, a grid originating from datum consisting of 5-by-5-foot squares oriented north and south was laid out over each site. An English, as opposed to a metric, scale was utilized because of the nature of the materials being investigated. The grid enabled the location of each artifact to be mapped precisely as it was discovered during the course of excavation. By studying the way in which these artifacts are distributed across the site in relation to site stratigraphy, archaeologists are frequently able to determine what, where, and when various activities took place. In order to define site stratigraphy, 2-1/2-foot-wide test trenches were excavated by hand at sites 42To468, 42To469, and 42To470 to define site stratigraphy. Exposed stratigraphy was mapped, photographed, and sampled for analysis by USDA soil scientists.

Figure 15. All-terrain vehicle used for transporting personnel and equipment.

The test trenches revealed that all artifacts from undisturbed contexts were deposited on a single level that consisted of the interface between the sand dunes which covered the sites and the underlying playa. Small items such as percussion caps and pins, which might normally have fallen through 1/8" screen, were exposed in situ. Based on the testing results, a decision was made to dispense with the screening process and its associated time-consuming operation of transporting the excavated back dirt to water. Instead the dune was simply stripped off with trowels, brushes, and dental picks (Figure 16). In most instances, the bottom lenses of wind-deposited dune sand simply "popped" off, exposing the artifacts in situ. After being exposed in place, the artifacts were mapped, photographed, and removed. Upon removal, artifacts and their associated matrix were packed for transport in polyethylene bags. The bags were then transported by all-terrain vehicle trailer to trucks at Floating Island, on to the Department of Transportation maintenance shed at Wendover, and finally to the division laboratories in Salt Lake City.

Figure 16. Excavation at one of the wagon sites.

LABORATORY METHODS

After arrival at the division laboratories, the artifacts were sorted by material type in preparation for cleaning, stabilization, restoration, documentation, and identification. Perishable specimens were stored under refrigerated conditions in sealed fumigated containers.

Glass and ceramic fragments were removed from their bags and cleaned in deionized water. A backing of yellow enamel was applied. Field specimen numbers were inked onto the enamel and sealed with clear lacquer. Glass fragments were cross mended with Evercoat Epoxy Super Glue. Ceramics were cross mended with Duco Cement. Composite vessels were illustrated with scale drawings, and wood was photographed.

Brass artifacts were removed from field bags and the matrix was removed with water and camel-hair brushes. Specimens were photographed with color slides. Specimens were then cleaned with a jet air abrasive utilizing glass beads to remove the oxidizing elements. Scratches, wear marks, motifs, machine marks, maker's marks, and other distinctive markings were noted. Specimens were drawn to scale and photographed. Brass artifacts are stored in labeled chipboard trays or fastened to labeled string tags.

Iron specimens were removed from their field containers and encapsulating soil was removed using dental picks and camel-hair brushes. Specimens were photographed and then x-rayed by the staff of LDS Hospital Radiology Department (Figure 17). Exposures varied from 0.07 seconds at 140 KV and 50 MA to 2 seconds at 140 KV and 100 MA. Most exposures were sufficient to allow for identification of the artifact and scale drawings to be made. X rays also indicated that 99 percent of the iron specimens were totally oxidized, thereby rendering the traditional method of cleaning by electrochemical reduction useless. Specimens not identified by X rays were sectioned with a rock saw (Figure 18). Scale drawings were made from the cross sections.

Field specimen #214 was used as a test sample for the treatment of leather specimens recovered during the course of the project. The specimen was removed from its field container and observed under a binocular microscope with magnification of 0.7x20 and a variety of filters. A blue filter gave the best detail. After being observed under the microscope, a 1 cm sample was extracted and immediately submerged in reagent-grade alcohol where it became very brittle. The matrix of salt, mud, and burned charcoal embedded in the specimen was then removed with dissecting needles. After cleaning, the alcohol was removed from the sample, a paper towel serving as a blotter. Distilled water was introduced to the sample after which the sample flattened and softened, approximating its original condition. Alcohol was reintroduced to drive out the water and then removed. The sample was then consolidated with a 5 percent solution of acryloid B–67 isobutyl methacrylate polymer in acetone.

Wood fragments were removed from their sealed field containers and the loose soil in which they were packed to retain moisture content during transportation was removed with a camel-hair brush and dental picks. After cleaning, the samples were stored in labeled sealed polyethylene bags to prevent desiccation. Samples were photo-

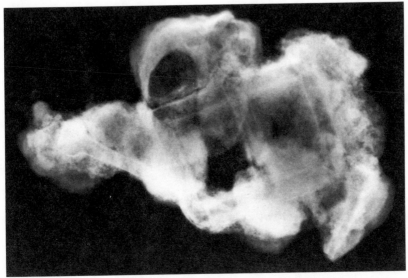

Figure 17. X ray of a typical iron artifact recovered from the wagon sites. Photo credit: LDS Hospital.

Figure 18. Cross section of a hollow auger encrustation cut with a rock saw.

graphed, and selected samples were illustrated to scale with accompanying notes. The specimens were then sent to the Department of Forest Resources, Utah State University, for identification by Dr. Richard F. Fisher. Genus-level identification was made for all samples, but due to fiber compression and decomposition, species-level identification was rendered difficult if not impossible.

After being photographed in their field containers, textile samples and their surrounding matrix were placed in a supportive net of fiberglass screen. The samples supported by the screen were then agitated in a solution of deionized water. After most of the matrix was removed, a plant sprayer filled with deionized water was used to rinse away the remaining matrix. The textile was then unfolded onto a supportive glass plate where it was observed and photographed under a microscope. The specimen was then placed into a sealed container with a fumigant and placed in a refrigerator until they could be forwarded to the Utah Museum of Natural History for detailed analysis by Ann Hanniball.

Faunal remains were in generally good condition and were processed in the laboratory by dry brushing and washing to remove embedded salts. An analysis of vertebrate bone was conducted by M. Elizabeth Manion in conjunction with James H. Madsen, Jr., the Utah state paleontologist.

Six

Archaeological Context

*T*he five sites, 42To467 through 42To471, identified during the course of the original Air Force survey are located on the mud flats of the Great Salt Lake Desert some 3.7 to 5.4 miles east-southeast of Floating Island. The sites are separated from each other by distances of 1/4 to 3/4 miles and contain wagon wheel ruts, small pits, wagon wheel tire stains, charcoal concentrations, and in situ scatters of artifacts. Sites 42To468, 42To469, and 42To470 were covered by low wind-deposited dunes which had formed to a height varying from 8 to 12 inches above the playa. Sites 42To467 and 42To471 were covered by a 3/4-to-2-inch mixture of wind-blown sediments mixed with playa clay. Pedestrian or vehicular activity was probably responsible for the mixed nature of these sediments. All sites had been disturbed during the recent past.

42To467

Site 42To467, the easternmost site, is in the NW1/4 of the SE1/4 of Section 26, Township 2 North, Range 15 West, Tooele County, Utah, at an elevation of 4216 feet. UTM (Universal Transverse Mercator) coordinates for the site are 4528760 northing 287645 easting. When initially encountered, this site consisted of four surface artifacts. The site measured 27.5 feet by 20 feet and covered an area of 30 square feet when fully excavated. It consisted of two parallel sand-filled wagon wheel ruts, a sand-filled pit, a wagon wheel tire stain, and a scatter of 62 artifacts, all of which were capped by a 1-to-2-inch layer of sand mixed with clay (Figure 19).

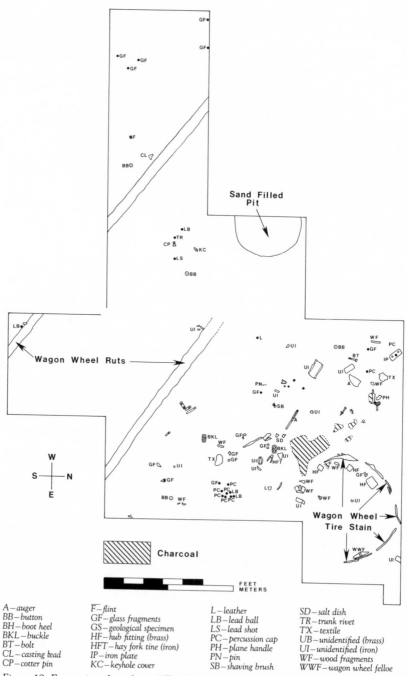

Figure 19. Excavation plan of site 42To467.

A — auger
BB — button
BH — boot heel
BKL — buckle
BT — bolt
CL — casting lead
CP — cotter pin

F — flint
GF — glass fragments
GS — geological specimen
HF — hub fitting (brass)
HFT — hay fork tine (iron)
IP — iron plate
KC — keyhole cover

L — leather
LB — lead ball
LS — lead shot
PC — percussion cap
PH — plane handle
PN — pin
SB — shaving brush

SD — salt dish
TR — trunk rivet
TX — textile
UB — unidentified (brass)
UI — unidentified (iron)
WF — wood fragments
WWF — wagon wheel felloe

The two wagon wheel ruts vary from 10 to 12 inches wide at the top and taper to a width of 10 inches at the base. The ruts originate from the playa surface and extend to a depth of 4 inches. The parallel ruts are aligned to 54 degrees west of north and are spaced 86 inches apart center to center. Both ruts are filled with wind-blown sand and capped by the surface mixture of sand and clay.

A bowl-shaped pit was encountered in line with the easternmost wagon wheel rut. The 40-inch diameter pit originates from the surface of the playa, extends to a depth of 12 inches, and is filled with culturally sterile gypsum sand. The pit may represent a hole that was excavated to free a mired wagon. The stain from a 5-foot-diameter wagon wheel tire was encountered in the northeast corner of the site, 8 feet 2 inches northeast of the wagon wheel ruts. A wooden wagon wheel felloe and parts of a broken hub fitting were in association. Felloes, when assembled together, form the wooden outer rim of the wheel over which the iron tire is shrunk.

Artifacts contained in the scatter include: clothing remnants, a shaving brush, ammunition, tack, wagon parts, carpenter's tools, medicine bottles, luggage parts, an ink bottle, and miscellaneous items of hardware. The artifacts were scattered across the site generally in contact with the playa surface or the surface of the sand which fills the wagon wheel ruts. In a few limited instances, artifacts were encountered in the sand clay mix which caps the site or immediately below the surface of the playa, a situation probably resulting from pedestrian or vehicular action. The heaviest area of artifact concentration measures 14 feet by 7 feet and generally parallels the wagon wheel ruts on the northeast. Those artifacts in contact with the fill of the wagon wheel ruts suggest that the scatter was deposited a short time after the ruts were filled, perhaps as a result of looting by subsequent emigrant parties or explorers.

42To468

Site 42To468 is located 1/2 mile northwest of 42To467 in the SW1/4 of the NW1/4 of Section 26, Township 2 North, Range 15 West, Tooele County, Utah, at an elevation of 4215 feet. UTM coordinates for the site are 4529275 northing 286765 easting. The site consisted of a 21-foot-by-30-foot-8-inch-high oval-shaped dune (Figure 20) when initially encountered. The perimeter of the dune was surrounded by a band of unidentifiable exfoliated fragments of iron. Two parallel wagon wheel ruts (Figure 21) were located at the northern boundary of the site.

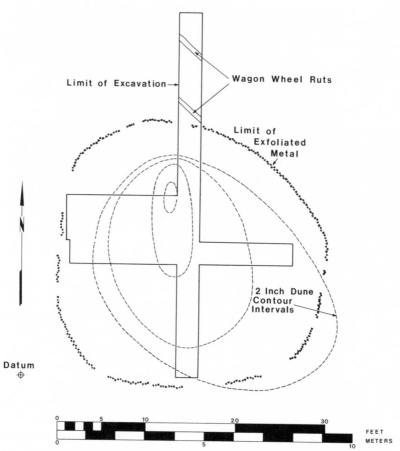

Figure 20. Topographic plan of site 42To468.

The wagon wheel ruts originate from the playa surface and extend to a depth of 5 1/2 inches. They vary from 6 to 9 inches wide at the top and taper to 4 inches wide at the base. The parallel ruts are aligned to 58 degrees west of north and are spaced 58 inches apart center to center. The ruts are filled and covered by wind-blown sand.

The remainder of the site was largely destroyed. Fifty-seven percent of the 112 square feet excavated had been disturbed by intrusive pits. The pits which originated at the surface of the dune had been excavated through the dune and into the underlying playa (Figure 22). A comparison of landmarks from photographs taken by Charles Kelly in 1929 (see Figures 5 and 6) suggests that 42To468 was one of

Figure 21. Wagon wheel ruts from site 42To468.

the sites which he investigated. As the photograph illustrates, a wagon axle was located at the site partially covered by the dune. The axle (Figure 23) is on exhibit at the Donner-Reed Memorial Museum in

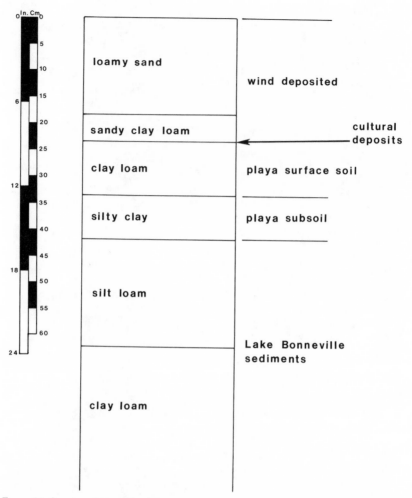

Figure 22. Stratigraphic profile of site.

Grantsville, Utah. Cellophane candy wrappers encountered in the fill of an intrusive pit located 16 feet north and 7 feet east of datum suggest that this site was also visited by the members of the Henry J. Webb expedition of 1962. Additional excavation at this site was considered pointless in view of the disturbance encountered. No artifacts were recovered.

Feet
Meters

Figure 23. Wagon axle, Donner-Reed Memorial Museum Collection, Grantsville, Utah.

42To469

42To469 is located 7/8 mile northwest of site 42To468 in the SE1/4 of the SW1/4 of Section 22, Township 2 North, Range 15 West, Tooele County, Utah, at an elevation of 4215 feet. UTM coordinates for the site are 4530015 northing 285530 easting. The site was covered by an oval-shaped 4-to-12-inch-high sand dune (Figure 24) measuring 28 feet by 72 feet. The dune was surrounded by a band of unidentifiable exfoliated iron fragments when first encountered. With the exception of disturbances on the north and south ends, the site was largely intact. 42To469 contained two sand-filled wagon wheel ruts, a large charcoal concentration, a small charcoal and ash stain, and a scattering of 121 artifacts (Figure 25), all of which were covered by the dune.

The two parallel wagon wheel ruts were aligned to 63 degrees west of north and were spaced 59 inches apart center to center. The ruts originate from the playa surface and extend to a depth of 3 inches. Width of the ruts varied from 4 to 8 inches at the top and tapered to 4 inches wide at the base. Both ruts were filled by wind-blown sand and were covered by the dune.

A large concentration of charcoal was discovered 9 feet south of the wagon wheel ruts and 23 feet east of datum. The east-west–oriented concentration measured 9 feet by 3 feet and contained fragments of partially burned spruce planks and unidentifiable iron objects. Heavy disturbance in the form of intrusive pits was encountered on the east and south sides of the concentration, effectively truncating the feature. Large quantities of charcoal encountered in the disturbed deposits suggest that the charcoal concentration may have extended to a length of between 14 and 17 feet at one time. The char-

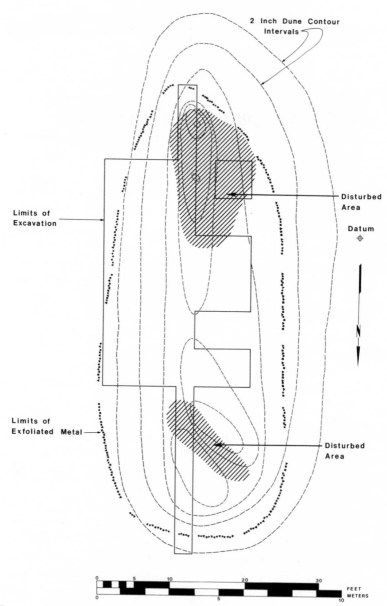

Figure 24. Topographic plan of site 42To469.

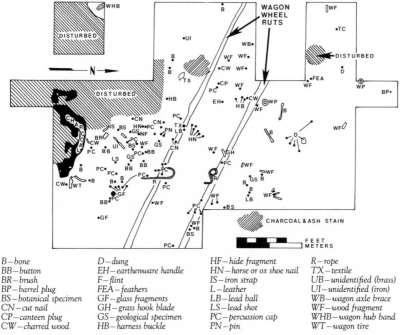

B – bone	D – dung	HF – hide fragment	R – rope
BB – button	EH – earthenware handle	HN – horse or ox shoe nail	TX – textile
BR – brush	F – flint	IS – iron strap	UB – unidentified (brass)
BP – barrel plug	FEA – feathers	L – leather	UI – unidentified (iron)
BS – botanical specimen	GF – glass fragments	LB – lead ball	WB – wagon axle brace
CN – cut nail	GH – grass hook blade	LS – lead shot	WF – wood fragment
CP – canteen plug	GS – geological specimen	PC – percussion cap	WHB – wagon hub band
CW – charred wood	HB – harness buckle	PN – pin	WT – wagon tire

Figure 25. Excavation plan of site 42To469.

coal concentration intruded through a 5/8-to-1-inch layer of sand which formed the lowest deposit of the dune which covered the site and was in contact with the playa surface.

A charcoal and ash stain measuring 2 feet 6 inches by 2 feet 2 inches was located between 3 and 6 feet north and between 25 and 27 feet east of datum adjacent to the southwesternmost wagon wheel rut. The stain was covered by the dune and was in contact with the playa surface. Portions of the fill of the southwesternmost rut covered the stain. Numerous partially burned small fragments of wood were associated with the stain. The discontinuous sand layer which formed the lowest dune deposit over much of the site was not present in this area.

Artifacts contained in the scatter include buttons from both military and domestic clothing, textiles, brushes, wire decorative devices, pins, percussion caps, lead balls and shot, flints, harness buckles, horse or ox shoe nails, rope, a broken axle brace, wagon-wheel tire remnants, wooden barrel and canteen plugs, a mug or jug handle, one-half of a medicine bottle, cut nails, wood fragments, and geological samples. The artifacts were scattered across the site in contact with a 5/8-to-1-inch discontinuous layer of sand, the playa surface or the fill of the wagon wheel ruts in areas where the sand deposit was absent. The sand deposit formed the lowest layer of the dune which covered the site and was in contact with the playa surface. The formation of the sand layer and filling of the wagon wheel ruts prior to artifact deposition suggests that the artifacts were deposited a short time after the ruts were filled. The heaviest concentration of artifacts measured 10 feet by 12 feet and was confined to an area between the wagon wheel ruts and the charcoal concentration.

42To470

Site 42To470 is the closest site to Floating Island and is located 1/3 mile northwest of site 42To469 in the NW1/4 of the SW1/4 of Section 22, Township 2 North, Range 15 West, Tooele County, Utah. Elevation is 4215 feet. UTM coordinates for the site are 4530290 northing 285110 easting. When discovered in 1986, the site consisted of a horseshoe-shaped 10-inch-high sand dune that measured approximately 35 feet by 60 feet. The perimeter of the dune was encircled by a band of unidentifiable exfoliated iron fragments (Figure 26). One hundred seventy-five square feet of the site was excavated. Ninety-three percent of this area had been heavily disturbed by intrusive pits which originated at the surface of the dune and extended beneath the surface of the playa. Three bones and a wagon bolster stake were recovered in contact with the remaining undisturbed playa surface (Figure 27). Additional excavation of this site in light of the extensive disturbance was considered pointless. The intrusive pits resulting from relic hunting remove archaeological materials from their original context and make historical interpretation difficult, if not impossible. No significant deposits were considered likely to remain.

42To471

42To471 is located approximately 350 feet northwest of site 42To469 in the SE1/4 of the SW1/4 of Section 22, Township 2 North, Range 15 West, Tooele County, Utah, at an elevation of 4215 feet. UTM coordinates for the site are 4530045 northing 285465 easting. When

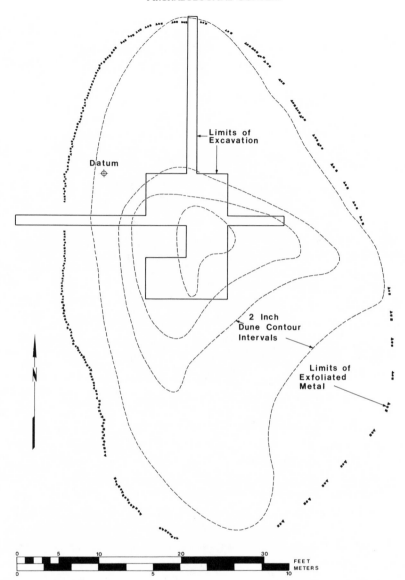

Figure 26. Topographic plan of site 42To470.

first encountered, the site consisted of an oval-shaped band of unidentifiable exfoliated iron fragments measuring 28 feet by 21 feet (Figure 28). Excavation revealed the remnants of a wagon wheel tire, a teardrop-shaped pit, and a wagon wheel hub fitting in contact with the playa surface (Figure 29).

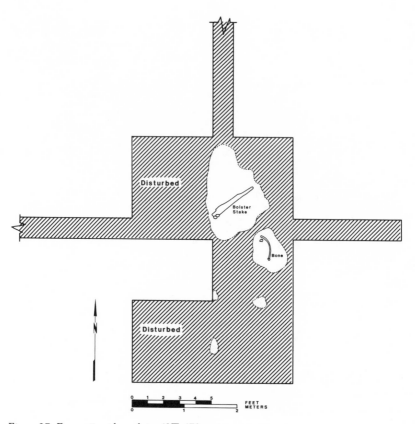

Figure 27. Excavation plan of site 42To470.

The wagon-wheel tire remnants consisted of a circular rust stain measuring approximately 55 inches in diameter. The stain contained the exfoliated remnants of an iron wagon wheel tire. The stain measured 4 inches wide by 1 inch high and was in contact with the playa surface. The totally oxidized remnants suggest that they had been slightly disturbed from their original context. Some of the remnants were positioned vertically and others lay horizontally. The rust stain and its associated tire remnant were covered by a 1/2-to-2-inch layer of sand.

The teardrop-shaped pit was located in the center of the wagon tire stain. The pit originated from the surface of the playa and extended to a depth of 6 inches. The pit measured 32 inches by 22 inches and was filled with a mixture of sand and clay which contained numerous

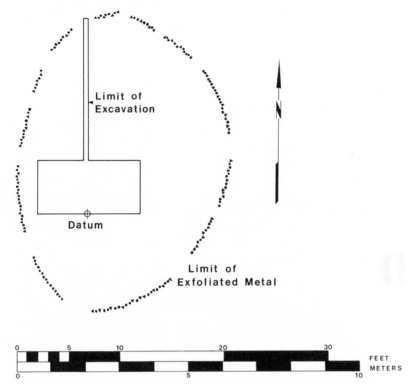

Figure 28. Preexcavation plan of site 42To471.

wood fragments and was stained by rust. The location of the pit and the material contained within its fill suggest that the pit once contained the hub of a wagon wheel which sometime during the recent past was removed along with its associated spokes and the wooden members of the wheel associated with the iron tire.

SUMMARY AND INTERPRETATION

Three of the five excavated sites provide a sufficient array of data to allow some interpretation. The spacing of the wagon ruts at the three sites are quite informative even without artifactual data. Wheel spacing at sites 42To468 and 469 is 58 and 59 inches respectively, a size that is quite consistent with that of most light farm wagons commonly used along the Oregon and California trails in the midnineteenth century. The 86-inch-wide spacing of the wagon tracks at 42To467 is sig-

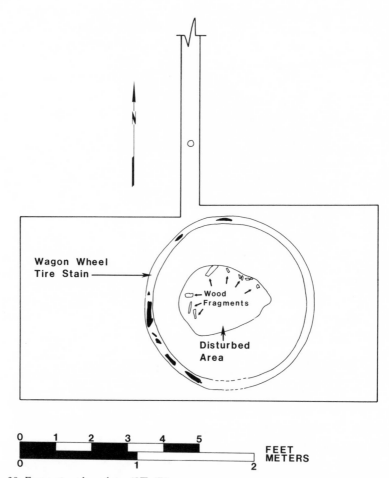

Figure 29. Excavation plan of site 42To471.

nificantly larger, and the diameter of the wagon wheel also exceeds
the size of provenienced wagons from the Oregon Trail. These outsized measurements suggest the ruts may well have been made by James
Reed's Pioneer Palace, a possibility that is quite consistent with the
large and diverse array of artifacts at the site. The items themselves
are typical of those carried by emigrants traveling the Oregon Trail in
the 1840s (Horn 1974:102–3). The sand-filled pit, through which one
of the ruts passes, appears to predate any of the expeditions to the
Donner-Reed wagons and may well represent an attempt to free the

wagon after it became mired in the playa mud. The distribution of ruts, pit, and artifacts is consistent with Reed's journal entries which indicate he returned to the salt flats and salvaged the Pioneer Palace after having left "everything but provisions, bedding, and clothing." In short, the shaving brush at 42To467 is probably that of James Frazer Reed, but the site may not be the location of an abandoned wagon.

Data from 42To469 is the most complex of any of the five excavated, but is correspondingly more interesting. The large bovid bones and the green bottlefly pupae casts suggest that at least one and possibly several oxen gave out and died at the site. The width of the wheel ruts and the large concentration of charcoal suggest that a light farm wagon was abandoned at the spot and subsequently burned. These features and a number of the artifacts recovered (such as the wheel hub band, the brush, and the earthenware fragment) are consistent with the interpretation that this site represents one of the abandoned Donner-Reed wagons.

A variety of other features suggest that the artifacts at the site are a palimpsest derived from a number of separate events. The geological specimens, horse or mule bones, buttons from military tunics, a military musket cap and ball, and horse/mule harness buckles are all strongly suggestive of a deposition at the site subsequent to that made by the Donner-Reed party. Harness tack is not used to rig ox yokes to wagons, and the Donner-Reed party exclusively employed oxen to haul their wagons. As a result, the harness buckles appear out of place unless they were either associated with a later depositional event, were packed for use in California, or are associated with an unrecorded use of mules. Hardesty (1987) has identified mule bones in the Donner-Reed party's winter campsites near Donner Lake, suggesting the latter possibility.

Geological specimens found at both 42To467 and 469 are derived from strata exposed on the north and west sides of the Great Salt Lake Desert and, hence, would not have been collected by a party traveling west. More likely, they represent material collected and discarded during a stopover at the site of an abandoned wagon by a party traveling east. The military buttons and expended percussion caps from the two sites are also more likely to be associated with a military expedition than with a civilian emigrant party.

Two such expeditions are known to have traveled east across Hastings Cutoff shortly after the Donner-Reed party abandoned several wagons in the mud flats. Captain Howard Stansbury's scientific exploration party and Captain James Brown's Mormon Battalion party are both known to have camped at the site of an abandoned wagon and used wagon parts to fuel their campfires. Since Stansbury collected a variety of scientific specimens including geological samples, it seems most likely that the specimens at 42To467 and 469 represent discards from Stansbury's collection, and that many of the other seemingly out-of-place artifacts may be related to Stansbury's expedition as well. That does not preclude some of them being related to the Brown party, however.

In sum, the greatest amount of information comes from sites 42To467 and 42To469. Site 42To468 contained identifiable wagon ruts and little else, but appears to be the location of a wagon collected by Charles Kelly. Site 42To470 was also highly disturbed and contains virtually no decipherable information. Site 42To471 appears to be limited to what remains of a wagon wheel. Its proximity to 42To469 suggests it may be related to activities at that site.

Seven

Artifacts

A wide array of artifacts, including clothing-related items, a shaving brush, ammunition, tack and animal equipment, wagon parts, tools, containers, geological specimens, wood samples, and miscellaneous items of hardware were recovered from three of the five wagon sites (Table 1). One hundred eighty-four artifacts, fifty-seven bones, and three dung boluses were recovered. The majority of these were from 42To469 (121) and 42To467 (62). Only one artifact came from 42To470. Artifact attributes suggest that all date from the first half of the nineteenth century, and the collection is consistent with other descriptions of material carried by pioneers of that era (Horn 1974).

CLOTHING-RELATED ARTIFACTS

A minimum of six articles of clothing are represented by the buttons, textiles, boot or shoe remnants, decorative devices, and straight pins collected from the sites. Articles represented include a military frock coat, a boot, a dress, a leather carrying case, overalls, and flannel drawers or shirts.

Buttons

Ten buttons were collected from sites 42To467 and 42To469. The collection from site 42To469 included one U.S. Army artillery button, one U.S. Navy or Marine Corps button, one undecorated brass button, two bone buttons, and one white glass button. The U.S. Army artillery button is a large-size (13/16-inch diameter) two-piece brass button with a shank attached to the back (Figure 30h). The

TABLE 1. Artifact Provenience

Artifacts	Sites			Totals
	42To467	42To469	42To470	
Clothing-Related	9	11	0	20
Buttons	4	6	0	10
Military	1	2	0	3
Other Brass	2	1	0	3
Bone	1	2	0	3
Glass	0	1	0	1
Textiles	2	2	0	4
Leather	2	0	0	2
Boot Heel	1	0	0	1
Carrying Case	1	0	0	1
Decorative Devices	0	1	0	1
Pins	1	2	0	3
Brushes	1	1	0	2
Ammunition	17	24	0	41
Percussion Caps	9	20	0	29
Fired	1	13	0	14
Unfired	8	7	0	15
Lead Balls	4	2	0	6
0.38 Caliber	2	0	0	2
0.39 Caliber	1	0	0	1
0.45 Caliber	0	1	0	1
0.64 Caliber	1	1	0	2
Lead Shot	2	1	0	3
0.30 Caliber	0	1	0	1
0.18 Caliber	1	0	0	1
0.21 Caliber	1	0	0	1
Flints	1	1	0	2
Bulk Casting Lead	1	0	0	1
Tack and Animal Equipment	3	20	0	23
Harness Buckles 2" x 1 1/2"	0	4	0	4
Horse/Ox Shoe Nails	0	13	0	13
Lengths of Rope	0	2	0	2
Buckles 3 5/8" x 1 7/8"	2	0	0	2
Harness Straps	1	0	0	1
Ox Bow Remnants	0	1	0	1
Wagon Parts	4	6	1	11
Grease Seals	0	1	0	1
Iron Rings	0	1	0	1
Axle Braces	0	1	0	1
Wagon Tire Fragments	0	2	0	2
Hub Bands	0	1	0	1
Hub Fittings	1	0	0	1

TABLE 1. Artifact Provenience (Continued)

Artifacts	Sites			Totals
	42To467	42To469	42To470	
Felloes	1	0	0	1
Bolts	1	0	0	1
Spikes	1	0	0	1
Bolster Stake	0	0	1	1
Containers	5	6	0	11
Medicine Bottles	1	1	0	2
Salt Dishes	1	0	0	1
Mugs and Jugs	0	2	0	2
Canteen Plugs	0	2	0	2
Barrel Bungs	0	1	0	1
Ink Bottles	1	0	0	1
Unidentified Bottles	2	0	0	2
Luggage Hardware and Pack-				
ing Containers	2	1	0	3
Trunk Keyhole Covers	1	0	0	1
Trunk Rivet	1	0	0	1
Crate Remnant	0	1	0	1
Tools	7	1	0	8
Grass Hook	0	1	0	1
Augers	2	0	0	2
Plane Handles	1	0	0	1
Hay Forks	1	0	0	1
Unidentified	3	0	0	3
Miscellaneous Hardware	2	19	0	21
Triangular Sheet Iron	0	1	0	1
Cut Nails	1	17	0	18
Fire Steels	0	1	0	1
Right Angle Plates	1	0	0	1
Unidentified Iron, Brass, and				
Leather	6	11	0	17
Iron	4	6	0	10
Brass	2	1	0	3
Leather	0	4	0	4
Geological Specimens	1	7	0	8
Wood Samples	5	15	0	20
Totals	62	122	1	185

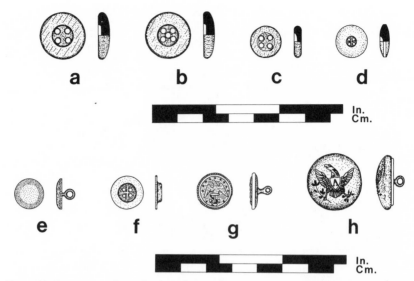

Figure 30. Buttons: a–c. bone; d. white glass; e. undecorated brass; f. four-hole brass; g. U.S. Navy or Marine Corps; h. U.S. Army artillery.

motif of a spread eagle and shield with the letter A in the center is the pattern authorized for wear between 1821 and 1851. The large size suggests that the button was worn on a frock coat. The button is back marked "Young & Smith Co./New York." Young & Smith Co. produced buttons from 1833 to 1844 (Luscomb 1967:225).

The U.S. Navy or Marine Corps button (Figure 30g) is a small-size (9/16-inch diameter) two-piece brass button with a shank attached to the back. The motif is that of an eagle perched on an anchor with its head cocked to the left. The eagle and anchor are encircled with eleven stars. The border of the button is in the form of cordage. Cordage and stars are separated by an undecorated circular band. The button is back marked "Wadhams & Co." Wadhams & Co. of Torrington, Connecticut manufactured buttons after 1847 (Luscomb 1967:212).

The undecorated brass button collected from 42To469 (Figure 30e) is a small-size (1/2-inch diameter) one-piece button with shank attached to the back. The face is slightly rounded and the button is back marked "*Birmingham*." Information regarding the manufacturer could not be located.

Two bone buttons from 42To469 are single-piece buttons with four holes in the center of the recessed front panel. One button is large (3/4-inch diameter) (Figure 30a) with a rounded back, while that of the small button is flat. Bone buttons such as these have been observed on overalls, wool flannel drawers, or with suspenders of the period.

The white glass button (Figure 30d) collected from site 42To469 is small (1/2-inch diameter) with curved faces front and back. One face exhibits a recessed panel in which four holes are centered. The button is otherwise undecorated and was probably part of a shirt or dress.

A U.S. Army artillery button, a single-piece undecorated brass button, a decorated two-piece brass button, and a bone button came from site 42To467. The artillery button, manufactured by Young & Smith Co., is identical to the specimen recovered from site 42To469. The bone button (Figure 30b) is also identical to the large-size bone button from 42To469 with the addition of a fifth hole added to the center for guiding the drill. The single-piece undecorated brass button (Figure 30f) is the small size (33/64-inch diameter). It exhibits a recessed panel through which four holes have been drilled. This button was probably worn on overalls or with suspenders. The two-piece decorated brass button is conically shaped and exhibits a floral motif (Figure 31). The button measures 3/8 inch in diameter and was probably worn on a dress.

Leather Boot Heel

The remnants of a leather boot heel (Figure 32b) were recovered from site 42To467. The remnants consisted of two 1-3/4-by-1-5/8-inch lamination fragments of 1/8-inch-thick leather. The fragments contained the cut and serrated edge of the heel insole and seven shoe nail holes. One hole contained the remnants of an iron nail.

Leather Carrying Case

The remnant of a long narrow leather carrying case (Figure 32c) was recovered from site 42To467. The case measures 9 inches long and tapers from a width of 2 7/8 inches at the top to 7/8 inch at the bottom. A double row of stitching holes borders the lower 7 1/2 inches of the case. Two 3/16-inch countersunk rivet holes are centered vertically in the top 1 1/2 inches of the case. The rivet holes are separated from the lower portion of the case containing the stitch holes by a stamped horizontal indentation. The case probably held a knife or some similar long narrow object.

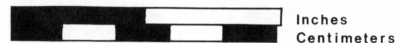

Inches
Centimeters

Figure 31. Brass button with floral motif.

Decorative Devices

One decorative piece of serpentine brass wire (Figure 33) was recovered from 42To469. The wire measures 1/4 by 3/4 inch and contained eyelets at each end. The type of garment to which the device was attached remains unidentified.

Pins

Three 1-1/8-inch-long brass straight pins were recovered. Two were recovered from site 42To469. One was recovered from 42To467.

Brushes

One brush (Figure 34) used in the application of shaving soap was recovered from site 42To467. The handle of the brush is missing, but the threaded horn receptacle and bristles are still intact. Bristles are from the domestic pig (*Sus* sp.). They form a bundle of fibers 3/4 inch in diameter and 1 3/4 inches long. The horn receptacle containing the bristles measures 1 inch long and has a 1/8-inch rim at the top.

One scrub brush (Figure 35) was recovered from site 42To469. The wooden back of the brush measures 3/4 by 2 1/4 by 5/16 inches and is oval shaped. Shallow channels have been tooled into the sides and a series of 1/4-inch holes have been drilled through the brush back. Bundles of over 2-inch-long doubled pig bristles have been placed into the holes. A thin wood veneer caps the holes on the surface of the back opposite the bristles. The bristles are pointed at the ends sug-

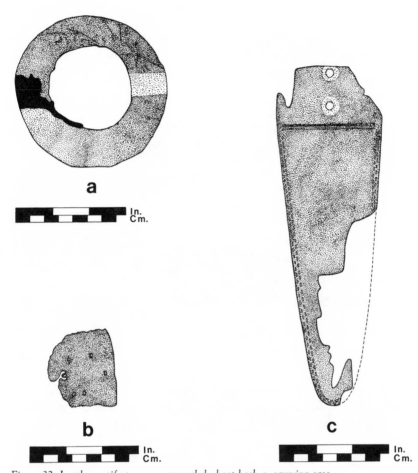

Figure 32. Leather artifacts: a. grease seal; b. boot heel; c. carrying case.

gesting that the scrub brush was new and unused at the time of abandonment.

Textiles

Textile remnants from 42To467 include two pieces of distinctly differing deep indigo blue dyed wool (see Appendix I). One specimen exhibiting a finely woven 2/1 twill weave appeared flat and ribbonlike upon initial examination. Very little of this specimen was extant and it shattered on contact. The other specimen measured 18.5 by 9.8 inches and exhibited a balanced plain weave with one felted or napped

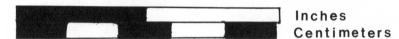

Inches
Centimeters

Figure 33. Brass decorative device.

Inches
Centimeters

Figure 34. Shaving brush.

surface. This specimen contained a seam sewn with plied silk thread. Textiles of this type were used in the production of military jackets and trousers of the period (Todd et al. 1974).

Two wool textile specimens were recovered from site 42To469. One measuring 1.5 by 1.7 inches was dyed a deep indigo blue. It was woven into a 2/1 twill weave with a nap of apparently undyed brown wool fibers. The other specimen was composed of single-ply brown and white wool threads woven into a 2/1 twill weave with a single reversal. The single reversal is probably the remnant of a wave or zig-zag pattern.

Figure 35. Scrub brush.

AMMUNITION

Ammunition for a minimum of one military musket, one shotgun, and two rifles or a pistol were recovered from sites 42To467 and 42To469. Weapons represented were muzzle-loading firearms utilizing both percussion and flintlock systems of ignition. Artifacts recovered include percussion caps, flints, lead projectiles (balls and shot), and bulk casting lead.

Percussion Caps

Twenty-nine percussion caps, nine from 42To467 and twenty from 42To469, were recovered. Fourteen of the twenty-nine had been expended during the course of discharging a weapon. Thirteen of the expended caps were recovered from site 42To469. One of the expended caps from site 42To469 was the type used with a large-caliber military musket. All other caps were of the size used with rifles, pistols, or shotguns.

Flints

Two flints used to discharge flintlock firearms were recovered from sites 42To467 and 42To469. The flint recovered from 42To467 measures 1/2 inch square. The flint recovered from 42To469 (Figure 36) measures 5/8 inch square. The size of both flints suggest that they were used with rifles or pistols (Lewis 1956).

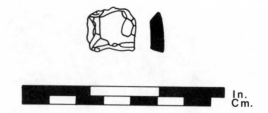

Figure 36. Rifle or pistol flint.

Lead Projectiles: Balls

Four basic sizes of lead musket, pistol, or rifle projectiles were recovered from sites 42To467 and 42To469. Caliber sizes include 0.38, 0.39, 0.45, and 0.64. Two 0.38-caliber balls, one 0.39-caliber ball, and one 0.64-caliber ball were recovered from 42To467. One 0.45-caliber ball and one 0.64-caliber ball were recovered from 42To469. The absence of rifling marks and other deformations suggest that none of the projectiles had been discharged from a weapon. The 0.38- and 0.39-caliber balls were probably used in civilian rifles. The 0.45-caliber ball could have been used in a civilian rifle or a Colt revolver.

Lead Projectiles: Shot

Three pieces of lead shot used in muzzle-loading shotguns were recovered from 42To467 and 42To469. One piece of 0.30-caliber shot was recovered from 42To469. One piece of 0.18- and one piece of 0.21-caliber shot were recovered from 42To467. The absence of deforming marks suggest that none of the shot was discharged from a weapon.

Bulk Casting Lead

One piece of bulk casting lead (Figure 37) was recovered from 42To467. The specimen is trapezoidal in shape, measuring 2 5/8 by 2 1/2 by 11/16 inches and weighing 1.00 pound. Casting marks are present.

TACK AND ANIMAL EQUIPMENT

Harness buckles, harness strap fragments, horse or ox shoe nails, rope, and the remnant of an ox bow comprise the artifacts included under the category of tack and animal equipment. Twenty of the twenty-three items of tack and animal equipment were recovered from site 42To469. The remainder came from site 42To467.

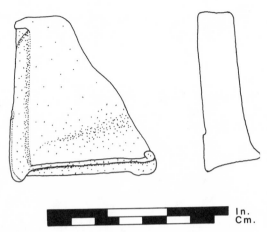

Figure 37. Bulk casting lead.

Four 2-by-1-1/2-inch harness buckles (Figure 38), 13 horse or ox shoe nails (Figure 39), the charred remnant of an ox bow, and two lengths of rope were recovered from site 42To469. Two fragments of tarred rope, measuring 36 and 45 inches respectively, were recovered from 42To469. The 1/2-inch-diameter multi-ply specimens were badly deteriorated, and the plant material from which they were manufactured could not be determined.

Two 3-5/8-by-1-7/8-inch buckles (Figure 43a) and one 3-5/8-inch fragment of a harness strap were recovered from site 42To467. The specific tack utilizing the buckles have not been identified. The harness fragment measures 1/4 inch thick and 11/16 inch wide. Two parallel rows of needle holes run across one end of the strap. Two parallel deep scratches angle across the strap on the rough side.

WAGON PARTS

Eleven wagon parts including a grease seal, an axle brace, wagon tire fragments, hub bands and fittings, a wheel felloe, a bolt, a spike, and a bolster stake were recovered from sites 42To467, 42To469, and 42To470. The presence of these wagon parts suggests that complete wagons were at one time associated with these sites.

Grease Seal

One leather grease seal (Figure 32a) was recovered from 42To469. The seal is circular and appears to have been cut by hand. The irreg-

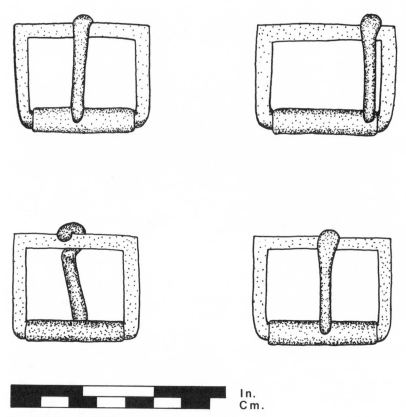

Figure 38. Harness buckles.

ular seal measures 4 inches in diameter and is 1/4 inch thick. A 2-3/8-inch hole has been cut in the center of the seal. Dried grease coats the rough side of the seal. A small portion of grease had leaked onto the smooth side. A 5/8-inch-wide indentation bisects the smooth side of the seal and may be the result of pressure applied by a linchpin.

Axle Brace

The broken remnant of an axle brace (Figure 40c) similar to one observed at the Donner-Reed Memorial Museum, Grantsville, Utah (Figure 41), was recovered from site 42To469. The brace exhibits a flattened diamond-shaped tip from which a 1/2-inch-diameter rod curves upward. A 5/8-inch-diameter bolt hole has been drilled through the diamond-shaped end of the brace.

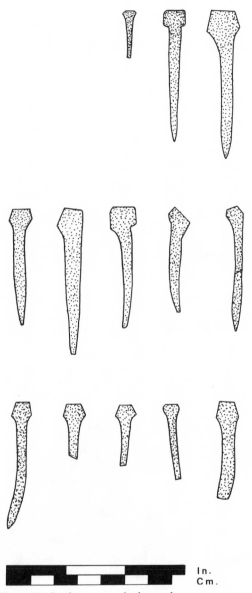

Figure 39. Ox, horse, or mule shoe nails.

Wagon Wheel Hub Bands, Wagon Tires, and Iron Rings
    Two badly deteriorated wagon tire fragments, an iron ring, and
the crushed band to a wagon wheel hub were recovered from site

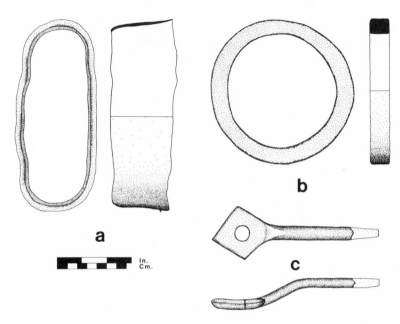

Figure 40. Wagon parts: a. crushed wagon wheel hub band; b. iron ring from a linchpin axle; c. broken axle brace.

Figure 41. Linchpin axle remnant with axle brace, Donner-Reed Memorial Museum Collection.

42To469. The crushed band (Figure 40a) measures 1/8 inch thick and 2 1/2 inches wide. Prior to being crushed, the hub measured approximately 7 inches in diameter. The iron ring (Figure 40b) is 3/4 inch thick and measures 5 3/4 inches in diameter. The center opening measures 4 1/2 inches in diameter. The iron ring was used to secure lengths of strap iron to the conical part of a linchpin axle. A similar ring serves that purpose on a linchpin axle remnant from the Donner-Reed Memorial Museum collection and on wagons provenienced to the Oregon Trail in the collections of the Oregon Historical Society and the Lane County Historical Museum.

Wagon Wheel Hub Box Fitting, Felloes, Bolts, and Spikes

A cast-iron hub box fitting, a white oak wagon wheel felloe (Figure 42), and a bolt and a spike (Figure 43b) were recovered from site 42To467. The hub box fitting (Figure 44c) is identical to those inserted into the rear of hubs that form part of the collection at the Donner-Reed Memorial Museum (Figure 45). Exterior dimension of the fitting taper from a 4-7/8-inch diameter to a 4-5/8-inch diameter. Interior dimensions expand from 3 1/2 to 4 inches in diameter. The 1/2-inch-diameter partially threaded bolt measures 2 3/4 inches long (Figure 43b).

Wagon Bolster Stake

The bolster and its two associated stakes were fastened to the axle and formed part of the frame which supported the wagon box. One wagon bolster stake (Figure 46) was recovered from site 42To470. The stake, which measures 26 inches long, is identical to one shown on a bolster collected by Dan Orr in 1930 (Figure 47). The 1-1/4-inch-thick oak bolster stake measures 3 3/4 inches wide at the base tapering to 1 1/2 inches wide at the top. A 1-by-3-1/2-inch rectangular notch has been cut into the base of the stake allowing it to fit into a slot in the bolster. One side of the stake is stepped and worn 4 3/4 inches above the notch and again 12 inches above the notch. The remnant of a bent iron strap is attached with bolts near the base. The strap would have fastened the stake to the bolster.

FOOD, WATER, MEDICINE, AND INK CONTAINERS

Artifacts representing a minimum of 11 glass, ceramic, and wood containers used for containing or serving food, water, medicines, and ink were recovered from sites 42To467 and 42To469.

Inches
Centimeters

Figure 42. Wagon wheel felloe remnant.

Ceramic Containers

A brown glazed earthenware mug handle and a single red earthenware jar fragment were recovered from 42To469. An undecorated white stoneware salt dish (Figure 48) was recovered from 42To467. The salt dish measures 2 3/8 inches in diameter, stands 3/4 inch high, and bears the impressed mark of "Zell." This mark was used on ceramics produced by J. F. Lenz at the Zell Pottery, Baden (Germany), between 1846 and 1867 (Cushion 1980:94).

Medicine Bottles

Two partial medicine bottles, missing shoulder, neck, and lip, were recovered from sites 42To467 and 42To469. The bottle recovered from 42To467 (Figure 49b) is octagonal with a base measuring 2 1/4 by 1 1/2 inches. The bottle is aqua in color and pontil scarred on the bottom. Mold seam marks suggest that it was manufactured in a two-piece mold. The bottle recovered from 42To469 (Figure 49c) is also aqua colored, pontil scarred, and manufactured in a two-piece mold. The bottle is cylindrical with a base diameter of 1 5/8 inches.

Ink Bottle

The partial remains of an ink bottle (Figure 49a) were recovered from 42To467. The octagonal bottle measures 2 3/16 by 2 3/16 inches and stands 2 1/4 inches high. The bottle is pontil scarred on the bottom. "M & P/New York" is embossed on two side panels. Only

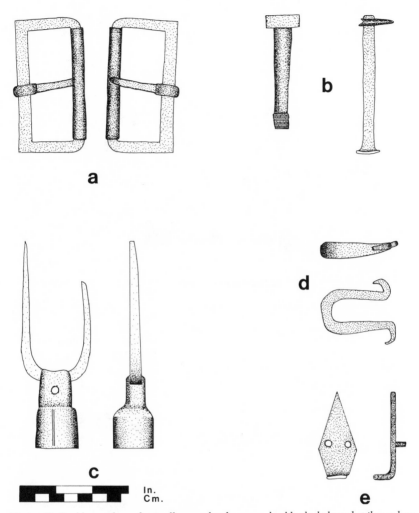

Figure 43. Buckles, tools, and miscellaneous hardware: a. buckle; b. bolt and spike; c. hay fork tine; d. fire steel; e. triangular sheet iron.

three companies bearing the initials M & P were listed in *Doggett's New York City Directory* between the years 1844 and 1850. McLeod & Pomeroy, bookbinders, were located at 150 Fulton Street. Manning & Pritchard, importers, were located at 54 Beaver. Moltz & Pollitz, commercial merchants, were located at 69 Broad.

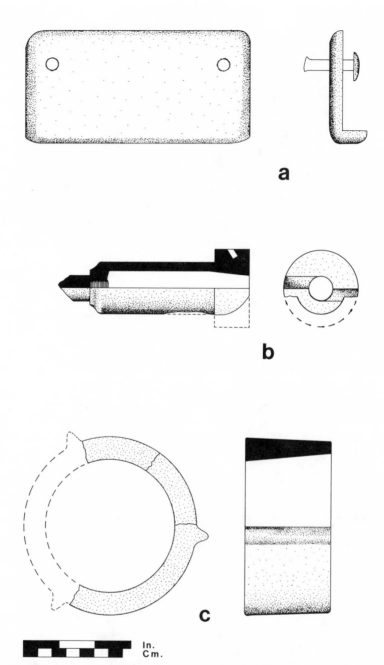

Figure 44. Wagon parts, tools, and miscellany: a. iron plate; b. hollow auger; c. wagon wheel hub box fitting.

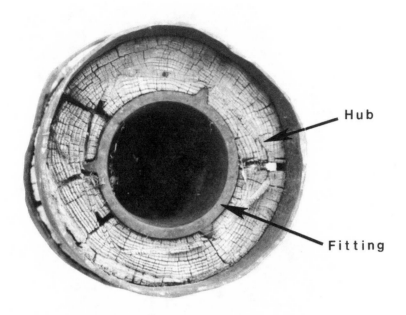

Figure 45. Wagon wheel hub with box fitting, Donner-Reed Memorial Museum Collection, Grantsville, Utah.

Feet
Decimeters

Figure 46. Bolster stake from site 42To470.

Unidentified Bottles

Four fragments representing a minimum of two unidentified bottles were recovered from 42To467. Two fragments represent a cobalt-blue-colored cylindrical bottle. One fragment (Figure 50) is an aqua-colored bottleneck with a hand-applied lip. The remaining fragment (Figure 50) is aqua in color and embossed " . . . . HIL."

Figure 47. Dan Orr holding a wagon bolster collected from a site near the "Birds Nests" ca. 1930. Photo credit: Utah State Historical Society.

Canteen Plugs and Barrel Bungs

Two white pine canteen plugs and one partial white pine barrel bung were recovered from site 42To469. Both canteen plugs (Figure 51) were probably used with the circular disk-shaped wood canteens of the period. Both plugs appear to have been whittled by hand and measure approximately 1/2 inch in diameter. One of the plugs exhibits a hole at the top through which a lanyard could be attached. The barrel bung (Figure 52) is hollow and cylindrical in form. The 2-1/2-inch-long, 1-1/4-inch-diameter bung steps down 1/4 inch 3/8 inch from one end so that it can be inserted to plug a 1-inch hole bored into the side or head of a barrel.

LUGGAGE HARDWARE AND PACKING CONTAINERS

A minimum of one trunk and one packing crate are represented by luggage hardware and packing container fragments recovered from

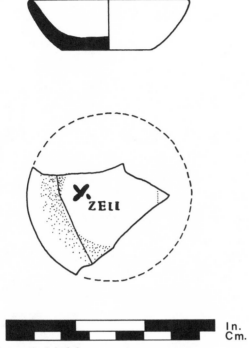

Figure 48. Salt dish.

sites 42To467 and 42To469. A brass trunk rivet and trunk keyhole cover (Figure 53b) were recovered from 42To467. The brass keyhole cover is identical to that shown on the trunk in photograph #1487 at the LDS Museum of Church History and Art, Salt Lake City, Utah. The keyhole covers on the 1848 medicine chest of Elijah Bristow and the 1840s trunk of James Clyman are also identical to the 42To467 specimen. The Bristow chest is in the collection of the Lane County Historical Museum, Eugene, Oregon. Clyman's trunk is at the Donner Memorial State Park, Truckee, California.

A 3/4-by-2-3/8-by-3/8-inch wood packing crate fragment was recovered from site 42To469. The fragment is mitered at one end. A nail hole runs through the mitered end.

TOOLS

Two agricultural tools, three carpenter's tools, and three unidentified tools were recovered from sites 42To467 and 42To469.

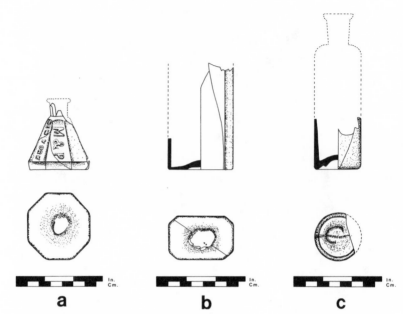

a   b   c

Figure 49. Glass bottle remnants: a. ink; b, c. medicine.

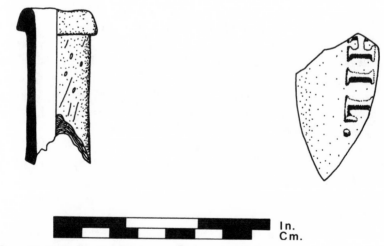

Figure 50. Bottle glass fragments.

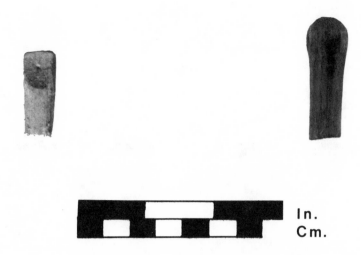

Figure 51. Canteen plugs.

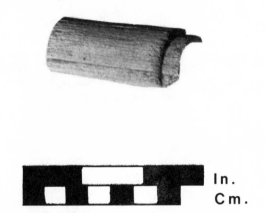

Figure 52. Barrel bung.

Agricultural Tools

One iron grass hook blade (Figure 54b) was recovered from 42To469 and one head from a two-tine hayfork (Figure 43c) was recovered from 42To467. The grass hook blade remnant includes the lower portion of the curved blade and the tang which fit into a wooden handle. Grass hooks were used like a sickle for cutting grass, hay, or other forage for animals.

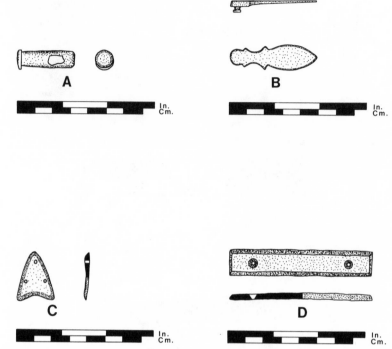

A

B

C

D

Figure 53. Brass artifacts: a, c, d. unidentified; b. keyhole cover.

Carpenter's Tools

One hollow auger (Figure 44b), one spiral auger (Figure 54c), and one plane handle fragment (Figure 54a) were recovered from 42To467. The hollow auger illustrated in the 1865 *Illustrated Catalog of American Hardware of the Russell and Erwin Manufacturing Company* (1980 edition) was used primarily for cutting tenons in mortise and tenon joints. The auger was designed for cutting a 5/8-inch-diameter tenon. It measures 4 7/16 inches long and contains the remnants of a threaded shaft. The spiral auger used in conjunction with a wooden handle measures 17 inches long and was designed to drill a 1-inch hole. The hickory plane handle is broken at the base. A portion of the handle top has been burned.

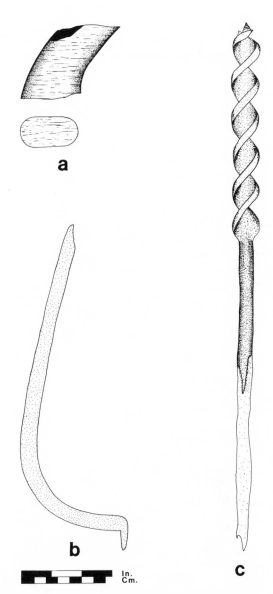

Figure 54. Tools: a. carpenter's plane handle; b. grass hook blade; c. auger.

Unidentified Tools

Three unidentified tools were recovered from 42To467. Two of the tools (Figure 55b, c) are identical and measure 6 5/8 inches long.

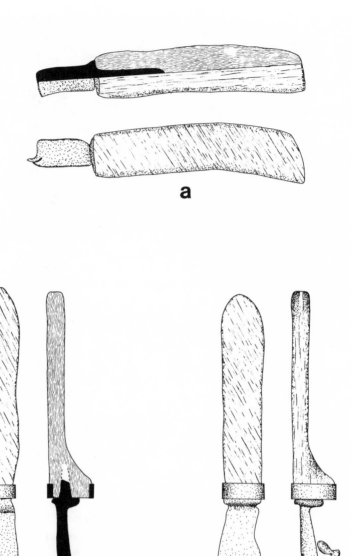

a

b

c

In.
Cm.

Figure 55. Unidentified tools.

They have a 1-inch-wide wood handle into which is fitted the tang from the unidentified iron portion of the tool. A 3/8-inch-wide, 1-inch-diameter brass band secures the iron to the handle. The third tool (Figure 55a) may be the remnants of a knife. It consists of a slightly curved 4-3/4-inch-long, 1-inch-wide Douglas fir handle into which is fitted the tang of an iron remnant which may represent a broken knife blade.

MISCELLANEOUS HARDWARE

A triangular piece of broken sheet iron, cut nails, a fire steel, and a right angle iron plate are included under the category of miscellaneous hardware. The triangular piece of sheet iron (Figure 43e) was recovered from site 42To469. It measures 2 1/4 by 1 inch and is bent and broken at one end. Two 1/2-inch-long pins protrude from the specimen.

Seventeen cut nails (Figure 56) were recovered from site 42To469, and one broken cut nail was recovered from site 42To467. Nails from 42To469 include two 4d, two 6d, and two 8d sizes. The remainder are unidentified fragments.

One fire steel (Figure 43d) was recovered from site 42To469. The fire steel was used in conjunction with a flint to create sparks which could ignite a fire. The fire steel measures 2 by 1 1/4 inches and has turned-up ends.

A flat right angle iron plate (Figure 44a) was recovered from site 42To467. The front of the plate measures 6 1/4 by 3 inches. The top measures 6 1/4 by 1 inch. Plate is 3/8 inch thick. Two 1/4-inch-diameter, 1-1/4-inch-long bolt remnants protrude from the rear through two holes in the plate.

UNIDENTIFIED IRON, BRASS, AND LEATHER

A total of ten unidentifiable iron specimens and four unidentifiable leather fragments were recovered from sites 42To467 and 42To469. Four iron fragments came from 42To467. Six came from 42To469. All four leather fragments came from 42To469.

Three brass specimens remain unidentified. Two specimens came from 42To467. One came from 42To469. The specimen from 42To469 (Figure 53c) is a 1/8-inch-thick triangular piece measuring 1 inch long and 7/8 inch wide. The specimen is slightly convex and has been ground around the edges, creating a beveled appearance. Three small nail or tack holes have been drilled through the specimen. The uni-

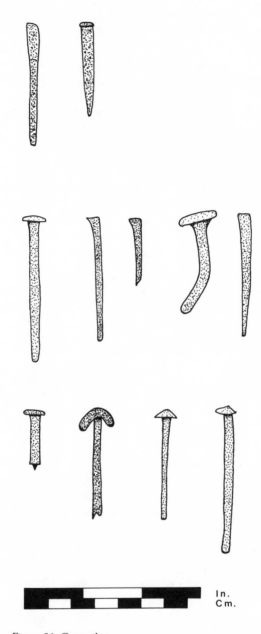

Figure 56. Cut nails.

dentified brass specimens from site 42To467 include a rectangular plate (Figure 53d) and an object resembling a cotter pin (Figure 53a). The rectangular plate measures 3 1/8 by 1/2 by 1/8 inches. Sides are beveled and two screw holes are countersunk into the plate at each end. One of the holes contains the remnants of an iron screw. The object resembling a cotter pin is cylindrical in shape measuring 3/8 inch in diameter and 1 1/4 inches long. It has a flat circular head that shows considerable signs of wear. Numerous machine marks are visible on the specimen shaft. A 3/8-inch-long slot runs through the center of the specimen shaft at the end opposite the head. The slot exhibits considerable signs of wear.

WOOD FRAGMENTS

A total of 20 wood fragments were collected from sites 42To467 and 42To469. Fifteen fragments came from 42To469. Five came from 42To467. Dr. Richard F. Fischer, Department of Forest Resources, Utah State University, identified the types of wood present in the collection. Genus-level identification was made for all of the samples, but due to fiber compression and decomposition that had occurred in many of the specimens, species-level identification was rendered difficult if not impossible. No clustering of wood fragments or wood types was noted for either site.

Wood types identified from site 42To469 included cottonwood/aspen, Douglas fir, hemlock, hickory, juniperus, spruce, walnut, and white oak. Spruce and white oak were most numerous followed by hickory and walnut, cottonwood/aspen, Douglas fir, hemlock, and juniperus. White pine, chestnut, Douglas fir, maple, and spruce were uniformly represented by the five fragments recovered from site 42To467. White oak, hickory, and maple were highly recommended for the construction of farm wagon running gear and axle beds (Adams 1981:203, 207). Spruce, a light tough wood recommended for the construction of boxes and crates (Brown et al. 1949:470), may have been used for building wagon boxes.

Ten of the fragments showed signs of milling. The others were either splinters or partially decomposed. Three milled surfaces were exhibited on a sample of white oak from site 42To469. Two flat milled surfaces measure 1 1/2 inches apart. A third milled surface is curved and contains the remnants of a broken nail. A hole has been bored through this surface. The size, curved surface, and location of the hole suggest that this fragment may have been part of a wagon wheel felloe.

A hickory fragment from the same site may represent the remains of a wagon cover bow. The fragment exhibits four milled surfaces and measures 1 1/2 inches wide by 3/8 inch thick. Two cut nail holes spaced 3 inches apart are centered longitudinally in the specimen. A third milled specimen from 42To469 is walnut. This fragment has four milled surfaces and measures 4 1/2 inches wide and 1 inch thick. Prominent saw marks are visible on the ends. A 3/4-inch-diameter hole has been drilled through the center. A spruce fragment from site 42To467, oval in cross section, may be the remains of a tool handle. The remaining milled samples have been milled flat on one surface only, the remainder having broken away or decayed.

GEOLOGICAL SPECIMENS

Eight geological specimens were recovered from sites 42To467 and 42To469. One specimen came from site 42To467. The remaining specimens came from site 42To469. Five of the specimens are cryptocrystaline quartz from outcrops of the Salt Lake formation. One specimen, a geode, is also from the Salt Lake formation. The remaining two specimens are quartzite. Specific source areas for the quartzite specimens could not be identified. Outcrops of the Salt Lake formation are located west and north of the sites in the Promontory Mountains, Raft River Mountains, and Pilot Mountains of northern Utah and Nevada.

FAUNAL REMAINS

Bones

Whole and fragmented remains of skeletal elements from at least three species were recovered from sites 42To467, 469, and 470 (Appendix II). Two bones representing *Bos/Bison* (probably oxen) were recovered from 42To467. The femur and vertebral body are both well preserved and are from a juvenile individual.

Nine *Equus* (horse/mule), seven *Bos/Bison* (probably oxen), seventeen unidentifiable large mammal bone elements, and two mammal bone fragments were recovered from 42To469. Ten additional elements were so poorly preserved they were recorded only as "bone splinters in mud." Identified elements were predominantly lower limb bones, vertebrae, and rib fragments. Six of the nine *Equus* elements represent the back left metacarpal/carpal complex of one individual. Three of the seven *Bos/Bison* elements were derived from the left forelimb of one individual. All *Bos/Bison* and *Equus* elements were from mature animals. The remains of a large juvenile mammal was represented by three vertebral body epiphyses.

The collection of nine bones from 42To470 is composed primarily of vertebra body/tail elements and rib fragments with a single horn core fragment. Only two could be identified to genus level, and both are from a juvenile *Bos/Bison*. A metacarpal from a bird (*Aves*) is believed to be incidental to the faunal collection.

Dung

Three samples of horse or mule dung were recovered from deposits in the northern part of 42To469. The dung boluses generally parallel the wagon wheel and are adjacent to the remains of a mature horse or mule. The dung consists of finely masticated grass, but the plant material is too finely ground to enable species identification.

SUMMARY

The material remains associated with the Hastings Cutoff wagon sites are all small and fragmentary, but still readily break down into two essential categories. (1) Wagon parts, animal tack, and household goods appear to be associated with a domestic emigrant party or parties traveling west along the trail. (2) The remnants of weapons, cloth, and buttons normally associated with military personnel, together with geological specimens from formations to the north and west of the Great Salt Lake Desert, suggest some remains were deposited by a military expedition traveling east.

Most of the artifacts cannot be positively associated with any one person or set of persons, but the integration of historical records with the material remains from the sites does allow some tentative correlations to be drawn. It seems likely that the shaving brush at 42To467 was that of James Reed and that most of the other domestic goods at the site were left by him and his family. The array of ammunition cannot be directly attributed to a military party, since many of the calibers represent weapons used by civilians. However, some, such as the 0.64-caliber balls used in military smooth-bore muskets, seem to be more likely from a military than a civilian party. The 0.45 ball could have come from either a rifle or a Colt revolver, but since Howard Stansbury is known to have carried a brace of Colt revolvers on his expedition around the Great Salt Lake, it is interesting to speculate that it came from his pistol.

EIGHT

Isolated Finds and
Previously Collected Artifacts

T he interpretation of the small, fragmentary remains recovered during the 1986 Silver Island Expedition can fortunately be supplemented by a variety of larger materials collected during previous expeditions. Artifacts were collected from Hastings Cutoff sites in the Great Salt Lake Desert in 1897, 1927, 1929, 1930, 1936, and 1962. Disposition of specimens collected during the 1897 expedition is unknown, but at least some of the artifacts from the 1927 Charles Davis expedition are on exhibit at Donner Memorial State Park in Truckee, California. The remainder may form part of the collection at Sutter's Fort State Park in Sacramento.

Artifacts collected by Charles Kelly, Frank Durfee, and Dan Orr during the 1929 and 1930 expeditions were deposited in an unspecified museum in Salt Lake City or with Grantsville High School. A review of the LDS museum and the University of Utah museum registration records list only one collection remotely associated with the Great Salt Lake Desert or any of the expedition members. Entry no. 2071 listed in the "Catalog of the LDS museum in the Bureau of Information" for June 11, 1943, lists a "large wagon in parts with wheels and tongue etc. which belonged to the Donner Party." The collection could not be located. Specimens from Grantsville High School have been transferred to the Donner-Reed Memorial Museum also in Grantsville. The collection presently includes over 40 specimens attributed to emigrant parties that traveled over the Hastings Cutoff. Only 27 of these items have documented provenience to the 1929 and 1930 expeditions or sites located along the cutoff.

Artifacts collected during the 1936 Walter Stookey expedition were allegedly deposited with the University of Utah museum prior to 1951. A pre-1951 photograph (Figure 13) shows Stookey with University of Utah President George Thomas in the museum next to a tableful of artifacts collected during the expedition. An examination of the museum accession records for the years 1930–56 failed to locate any entries for specimens shown in the photograph or donated by Walter Stookey. None of the specimens in the photograph form part of the existing collection.

Materials collected during the 1962 expedition are reportedly in the possession of J. Derle Thorpe, Logan, Utah (R. Tea 1986 personal communication).

Specimens from the 1927 Expedition at Donner Memorial State Park

A badly deteriorated rifle barrel, spokes, wagon wheel felloes, the remnants of two wagon wheel hubs, and the front platform or running gear to a wagon form the collection of specimens in the Donner Memorial State Park Emigrant Trail Museum collected by Charles Davis from the Great Salt Lake Desert in 1927. All wagon parts appear to be from light farm wagons whose wheels fasten to the axles with iron linchpins. The platform gear measures 59 by 37 by 10 inches. The felloe remnant attaches at the ends with wooden dowels. Spokes are fitted into holes drilled through the felloe at points one-third the distance from each end. Felloes measure approximately 2 inches wide by 1 1/2 inches thick.

Specimens from the 1929 and 1930 Expeditions at the Donner-Reed Memorial Museum

Provenienced specimens from the collection include wagon parts, ox yokes, barrel parts, rifle parts, ceramic tablewares, and storage vessels. The specimens were collected from a site thought to be 42To468 (Figure 5), a location near the Grayback Hills, and an unspecified location referred to in the literature as the "Birds Nests."

Location of the "Birds Nests" remained a mystery to us until we encountered a series of four bird nests perched atop 6-foot-high sand cones during a May 15, 1987, survey of the entire Great Salt Lake Desert portion of the trail. The nests were located in Sections 23 and 26, Township 1 North, Range 14 West, an area closely resembling the one described in Charles Kelly's *Salt Desert Trails*. A small surface site containing fragments of unidentifiable exfoliated iron and the fragment of a blue transfer-printed, scalloped-edge plate were observed in Section 26 during a reconnaissance in the fall of 1986.

Wagon Parts

Wagon parts from the collection include a bolster, a wagon wheel felloe, part of a rear axle, the remnants of a wagon box sideboard, part of a linchpin axle, and wagon wheel hubs.

The wagon bolster is the component which bolts to the axle and holds the wagon box in place. It consists of a wooden horizontal crosspiece and two wooden sidepieces or stakes. The Grantsville bolster (Figure 57) is provenienced to a site near the "Birds Nests." The bolster crosspiece measures 54 1/4 inches long. The center section of the crosspiece is rectangular in cross section, measuring 3 3/4 by 2 3/4 inches, 4 inches each side of center. A 1-inch hole for the kingpin has been drilled through the center of the crosspiece. A 2-inch-diameter hole has been countersunk 7/8 inch from the crosspiece base into the 1-inch hole. The crosspiece becomes rounded, tapering to a diameter of 2 1/2 inches toward the ends. Wear marks measuring 2 1/8 inches wide suggest that iron bands may have originally been placed over the ends of the crosspiece. A slot measuring 7/8 by 2 inches has been cut through each end of the bolster to hold the notched stakes. Two stakes, nearly identical to the specimen collected from site 42To470, are placed in each slot. The iron straps shown in the ca. 1930 photograph of the specimen (Figure 47) are missing. The stakes measure 25 inches long and 7/8 inch thick. They are 2 1/2 inches wide at the base necking down twice to a width of 1 3/4 inches at the top.

Wagon wheel felloes, when assembled together, form the outer wooden rim of the wheel over which the iron tire is shrunk. One complete wagon wheel felloe labeled "Hames found on the desert," forms part of the collection accumulated by the 1929 and 1930 expeditions. The curved wooden felloe measures 1 1/2 by 2 by 20 inches long. The felloe is doweled at each end. Two spoke holes placed 5 inches from each end are drilled through the felloe.

The partial rear wagon axle (Figure 23) from the museum collection was collected from a site believed to be 42To468. The 1929 Kelly expedition photograph (Figure 5) shows this specimen attached to another axle component eroding out of a dune. The wooden axle measures 58 3/4 inches long by 2 1/2 inches wide and varies between 3 and 3 5/8 inches thick. The axle tapers to a diameter of 2 1/2 inches

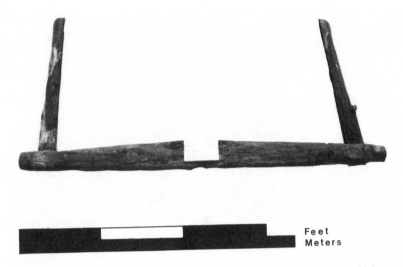

Feet
Meters

Figure 57. Wagon bolster from a site near the "Birds Nests." Donner-Reed Memorial Museum Collection, Grantsville, Utah.

at each end. Prominent ridges exist at the center and 15 1/2 inches each side of center. Notches measuring 1 3/4 inches wide by 1/2 inch deep have been cut into the ridges. The notches to either side of center contain 5/8-inch-diameter holes and are angled toward the center, suggesting that they once contained axle braces.

An unprovenienced 64-inch-long remnant of a dried-out bleached wagon box sideboard forms part of the museum's collection. The remnant measures 11 1/2 inches wide by 11/16 inch thick. Cut nail holes are placed 1 inch from the edge and 11 by 33 7/8 inches from the end of the plank. The remnant closely resembles a complete 8-foot-9-inch-long sideboard observed in Section 23, Township 1 North, Range 13 West.

The museum collection includes part of a linchpin wagon axle. Although unprovenienced, the axle deserves mention because of its associated parts. Similar parts were recovered from site 42To469, suggesting that this type of axle was used on wagons traveling Hastings Cutoff. The axle remnant is sawn off 30 inches from the axle end. The axle consists of a 6-by-5-inch rectangular piece of oak. The last 18 inches of the remnant have been turned to the shape of a cone. The cone-shaped portion of the axle tapers from a diameter of 4 3/4 inches to 3 inches. Three pieces of 1/8-by-2-inch strap iron have been bolted to the cone and secured by an iron ring and band. The iron ring is similar to a specimen recovered from site 42To469 and measures 6 1/2 inches in diameter and 5/8 inch thick. The center opening of the ring measures 4 3/4 inches in diameter. The iron band that secures the strap iron to the end of the axle measures 3/16 inch thick by 1 inch wide by 3 inches in diameter. A 1-by-3/4-inch slot in the band and axle holds an iron linchpin in place. A wooden bolster crosspiece and iron axle brace are bolted to the axle.

A number of wagon wheel hubs in various stages of deterioration form part of the museum collection. One of the hubs (Figure 58) was photographed on the mud flats during the 1929 expedition. The hub is formed from a solid piece of wood which measures 16 inches long. A hole tapering from 4 1/8 inches to 3 inches has been bored through the center of the hub. Iron box fittings similar to those recovered from site 42To467 are placed in each end of the hub. The exterior of the hub measures 7 1/8 inches in diameter necking down to 5 1/2 inches, 4 inches from the outside end. Fourteen 2-1/4-by-13/16-inch spoke holes have been mortised into the hub approximately 15/16 inch apart. Scribe lines marking the spoke hole locations are still visible.

Ox Yokes

Two ox yokes (Figures 59 and 60) from the museum collections were recovered from a site near the "Birds Nests" during the 1929 and 1930 expeditions. Figures 61 and 62 show the ox yokes shortly after their recovery.

Barrel Parts

A broken barrelhead (Figure 63) and a barrel stave (Figure 64) from the museum collection were recovered from a site north of Floating Island (Figure 7) during the 1929 expedition. The wooden barrelhead is constructed in three sections which have been doweled together. The 3/4-inch-thick head measures 18 1/4 inches in diameter. The edges of the lid have been beveled to a point. Beveled surfaces are irregular, suggesting that the surface was worked with hand tools. One surface of the head exhibits numerous cut marks (Figure 65), suggesting that the outer surface of the head doubled as a cutting board.

The slightly curved wooden barrel stave is bowed along its length. The stave measures 30 inches long by 3 1/8 inches wide by 1/2 inch thick. Both ends of the stave have been cut across the interior surface of the stave 5/8 inch and 1 5/16 inches from one end.

Feet
Decimeters

Figure 58. Wagon wheel hub collected from the wagon sites ca. 1930, Donner-Reed Memorial Museum Collection, Grantsville, Utah.

Feet
Meters

Figure 59. Ox yoke recovered from a site near the "Birds Nests," Donner-Reed Memorial Museum Collection, Grantsville, Utah.

Rifle Parts

The remnants of a stock and two badly rusted rifle barrels in the museum collection were recovered from a location near the

Feet
Meters

Figure 60. Ox yoke recovered from a site near the "Birds Nests," Donner-Reed Memorial Museum Collection, Grantsville, Utah.

Figure 61. Frank Durfee holding an ox yoke shortly after its recovery from a site near the "Birds Nests" ca. 1930. Photo credit: Utah State Historical Society.

117

Figure 62. Dan Orr holding an ox yoke shortly after its recovery from a site near the "Birds Nests" ca. 1930. Photo credit: Utah State Historical Society.

Grayback Hills. Both barrels are octagonal in cross section, and measure 1 inch and 7/8 inch across the flats respectively. One barrel is bent and measures 38 7/8 inches long. It has a 1/2-inch bore and contains a hole near the breech where the percussion cone was placed. The second barrel measures 29 5/16 inches long and is broken near the breech. Three 5/8-inch-long dovetails are placed along its base. Barrel bore is approximately 9/16 inch.

The wooden rifle stock remnant (Figure 66) contains a recessed notch and screw holes for the butt plate and a recessed cavity for a dome-shaped patch box hinge and lid. The patch box hinge was held in place with three screws.

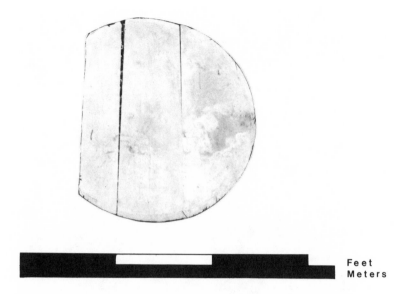

Feet
Meters

Figure 63. Barrelhead recovered from a site north of Floating Island, Donner-Reed Memorial Museum Collection, Grantsville, Utah.

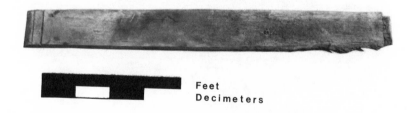

Feet
Decimeters

Figure 64. Barrel stave recovered from a site north of Floating Island, Donner-Reed Memorial Museum Collection, Grantsville, Utah.

Ceramics

Fragments representing a minimum of 16 ceramic vessels were recovered from a site near the "Birds Nests" by Clark, Durfee, and Frandsen. The collection includes three porcelain, six refined earthenware, and seven stoneware vessels.

One 8-1/2-inch porcelain plate (Figure 67), one 5-3/4-inch porcelain saucer (Figure 68a), and one porcelain teacup (Figure 68b) were collected from the "Birds Nests." The vessels, which appear to form

Figure 65. Closeup of barrelhead showing cut marks.

Feet
Decimeters

Figure 66. Rifle stock remnant recovered from a site near the Grayback Hills, Donner-Reed
Memorial Museum Collection, Grantsville, Utah.

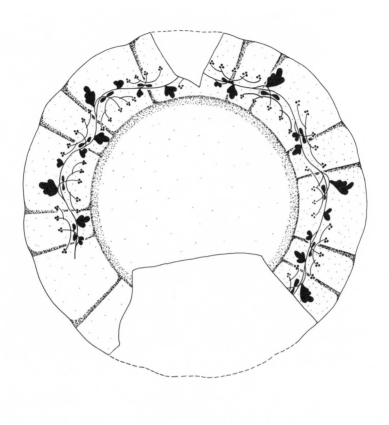

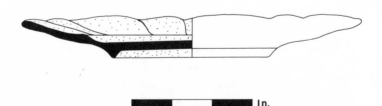

Figure 67. Hand-painted porcelain plate recovered from a site near the "Birds Nests," Donner-Reed Memorial Museum Collection, Grantsville, Utah.

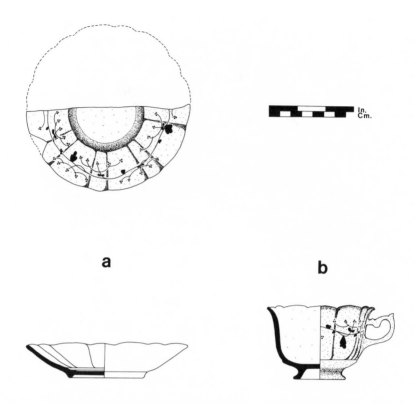

Figure 68. Hand-painted porcelain vessels recovered from a site near the "Birds Nests," Donner-Reed Memorial Museum Collection, Grantsville, Utah: a. saucer; b. teacup.

part of a single table setting, are decorated with a hand-painted motif of grapes, vines, and leaves applied over glaze. The grapes are blue, the vines reddish purple, and the leaves green.

The refined earthenware collected from the "Birds Nests" vicinity are pearlware vessels decorated with flown colors and scalloped and feather edging. One 11-1/4-inch octagonal plate (Figure 69c), one 6-1/2-inch scallop-edged plate (Figure 69a), one 6-inch saucer (Figure 69b), and one teacup are decorated with flown blue colors and floral motifs. The scallop-edged plate, saucer, and cup appear to be from a matching place setting.

Feather-edge decorated wares include a fragment representing a plate and the remnants of a platter (Figure 70). The plate fragment exhibits blue feather edging without relief, a decorative technique which developed after 1840 (Gram n.d., Branstner 1986).

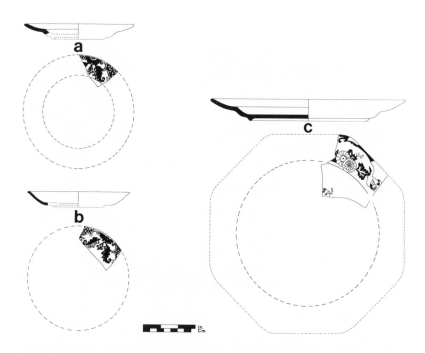

Figure 69. Pearlware vessels from a site near the "Birds Nests," Donner-Reed Memorial Museum Collection, Grantsville, Utah: a. plate; b. saucer; c. plate.

The stoneware collected from the "Birds Nests" includes fragments representing seven grayware storage vessels. Vessels represented include one jug, two jars, one crock, and the bases for three crocks, jars, or jugs. All vessels have been formed on a potter's wheel. Vessel form, particularly that of the jug, resembles vessels recovered from the Wilcox Pottery, Ontario County, New York. The Wilcox vessels date to 1850 (Barber and Hamell 1971). The jug (Figure 71), labeled "F.D.O. 14.11," exhibits an unglazed interior and salt-glazed exterior. One of the jars (Figure 72), labeled "F.D.O. 14.13," exhibits an unglazed interior and a brown salt glaze uniformly applied to the exterior. The exterior of the second jar is salt glazed, while the interior is covered with an Albany slip. The crock (Figure 73), labeled "F.D.O. 14.16," is decorated with two incised parallel bands encircling the vessel. The interior of the crock is unglazed. The exterior is covered with a nonuniformly applied brown salt glaze.

The three bases, one of which is labeled "F.D.O. 14.12," measure 4 3/8, 6 3/4, and 6 3/4 inches in diameter. All three of the bases

Figure 70. Scalloped feather-edge decorated platter from a site near the "Birds Nests," Donner-Reed Memorial Museum Collection, Grantsville, Utah.

exhibit a salt-glazed exterior. Two bases are unglazed on the interior. The interior of the third is covered with an Albany slip.

HASTINGS CUTOFF RUTS AND ISOLATED FINDS
In the absence of associated artifacts and/or careful excavation, it is impossible to distinguish the ruts of Hastings Cutoff from those made by twentieth-century vehicles. All ruts appear on the surface of the mud flats as discolored bands of soil which result from the wind-blown deposits that fill them. Local tradition holds that at least one set of the filled-in ruts emerging from the dunes northwest of Knolls, Utah, are those of Hastings Cutoff.

Reconnaissance conducted on May 12–14 and June 17–19, 1987, located one group of ruts that follow the route shown in Figure 74. These ruts contained early to mid-nineteenth-century artifacts. The ruts were followed from their emergence from the dunes in Section 21, Township 1 North, Range 14 West. From Section 21, the ruts continue west past the "Birds Nests" in Section 23, Township 1 North, Range 14 West, to Section 21, Township 1 North, Range 14 West. From this point, the ruts angle sharply northwest where they lead to sites 42To467–471. The ruts continue northwest from the sites, pass-

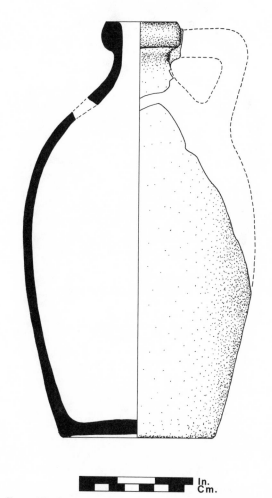

Figure 71. Grayware jug from a site near the "Birds Nests," Donner-Reed Memorial Museum Collection, Grantsville, Utah.

ing north of Floating Island before ascending out of the mud flats to Donner-Reed Pass. The route heads west from the pass to Pilot Springs.

Fragments from a sarsaparilla bottle, the base to a small medicine bottle, and 253 grayware ceramic sherds representing two earthenware jugs were recovered from or near the ruts during the reconnaissance. The embossed emerald green sarsaparilla bottle (Figure 75)

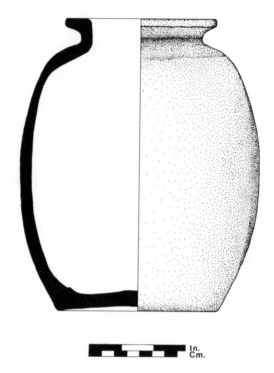

Figure 72. Grayware jar from a site near the "Birds Nests,"
Donner-Reed Memorial Museum Collection, Grantsville,
Utah.

measures 3 by 3 by 9 1/4 inches. It contained "Dr. Townsends
Sarsaparilla," a patent medicine product of Dr. Samuel P. Townsend,
Albany, New York. The presence of " . . . ANY/ . . . . Y." on a side
panel fragment of the bottle suggests that the bottle was manufac-
tured between 1839 and 1846 when Townsend operated out of Albany,
New York. Townsend moved his operation to New York City in 1846
(Fike 1987:220). The fragments of the bottle were embedded in the fill
of the ruts along a 350-foot stretch in Section 20, Township 1 North,
Range 13 West.

The aqua-colored rectangular medicine bottle base is pontil
scarred and beveled at the corners. The base measures 1 5/8 by 1 3/16
inches. The pontil scar suggests a manufacturing date prior to 1860.
The base was recovered from the fill of a rut in Section 21, Township
1 North, Range 13 West, approximately 1 mile east of the sarsaparilla
bottle fragments.

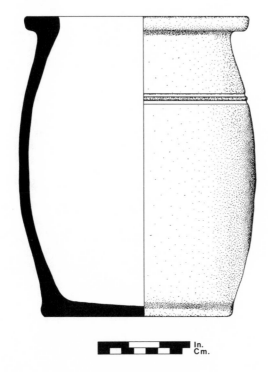

Figure 73. Grayware crock from a site near the "Birds Nests," Donner-Reed Memorial Museum Collection, Grantsville, Utah.

The jug fragments were recovered from the northwest 1/4 of the northeast 1/4 of the southwest 1/4 of the northeast 1/4 of Section 21, Township 1 North, Range 13 West, approximately 400 feet from the edge of the dunes. The sherds were in contact with the surface of the mud flats and were scattered over an area measuring 16 by 12 feet. The scatter fanned out south and east from the area of heaviest concentration. The area of heaviest concentration measured 4 feet 6 inches by 3 feet 6 inches and began approximately 2 feet 6 inches south of the ruts. One of the jugs exhibits an unglazed interior surface of red clay veneer. The exterior of the jug is covered with a brown salt glaze. The second jug is salt glazed on both exterior and interior surfaces.

SUMMARY

Artifacts in existing collections include some domestic goods, but consist principally of large, readily identifiable, and easily collected wagon

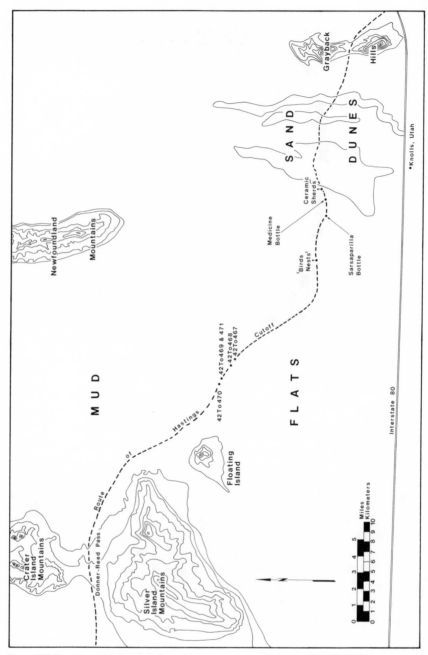

Figure 74. Location of isolated finds and wagon sites along Hastings Cutoff.

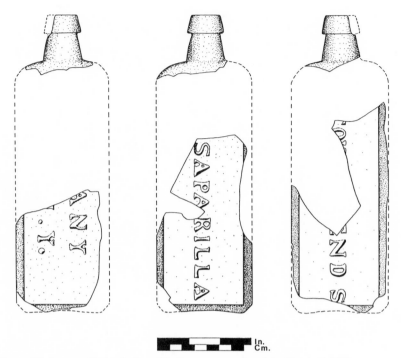

Figure 75. Sarsaparilla bottle from fill of wagon ruts west of the Grayback Hills.

parts. Some of these can be provenienced to sites 42To467–471 through photographic evidence, while others are clearly associated with Hastings Cutoff sites to the east and northwest. Most of these curated artifacts are derived from caches or abandoned wagons, but it seems clear that many objects were simply discarded on an individual basis along the way. It is unclear whether these represent discards by the original owner or goods plundered from caches and then thrown away.

NINE

Interpretation

*H*istoric archaeology along the Hastings Cutoff involves the interpretation of three differing kinds of information from which "best-fit" reconstructions and hypotheses can be drawn. These data are very different. A basic data source is, of course, the historic record derived from the journals and diaries of those who used the cutoff in the mid-nineteenth century. Equally basic is the physical record recovered archaeologically by the Silver Island Expedition. Since the ravages of more than a century of "collecting" left only the smaller physical remains, a third, albeit secondary and often less reliable, source of data was sought in poorly documented museum collections related directly to the Hastings Cutoff and to western settlement in general. Together these data are in some instances confusing and contradictory, but more often allow reconstruction that would be impossible from any one type of information alone.

Museum collections and historic records have been available for some time, and the new pieces to the puzzle are derived from the archaeological record. For that reason, we have attempted to clarify the nature of these remains within the context of these other source data. The five wagon sites investigated by the Silver Island Expedition are located along a 1.7-mile stretch of filled-in Hastings Cutoff wagon wheel ruts. Two sites, 42To468 and 42To470, were so heavily disturbed by previous expeditions that little remained. The remaining sites, however, contained wagon wheel ruts, identifiable stains of metal wagon parts such as wheels, wooden wagon parts, extensive concentrations of charcoal, animal remains, and a scattering of small early to mid-nineteenth-century artifacts separated from the surface of the desert by a thin layer of sand.

Comparison of the size, spacing, and orientation of the wagon wheel ruts allows some interpretation of the wagons responsible for creating them. Wagon wheel ruts were encountered at sites 42To467, 42To468, and 42To469. The ruts from 42To468 and 42To469 measure 4 inches wide at the base and are spaced 58 and 59 inches apart, suggesting that the same type of wagon was responsible for creating the ruts at both sites.

Wheel spacing represented by the ruts closely resemble that of running gear recovered from the Great Salt Lake Desert and of light farm wagons provenienced to the Oregon Trail between 1846 and 1852. Wheels on the front running gear of a wagon recovered from the salt flats by Charles Davis in 1927 are spaced 58 inches apart, while wheels on a wagon from the Oregon Historical Society which traveled the Oregon Trail in 1846 are spaced 60 inches apart. Wheels for the Reed wagon from the Lane County Historical Society which traveled the Oregon Trail in 1850 are also spaced 60 inches apart. Wheels for the Inman wagon, another vehicle from the Lane County Historical Society which traveled the Oregon Trail in 1852, are spaced 66 inches apart.

Tires from all vehicles measure between 1 1/2 and 2 inches wide, less than half the width of the ruts along Hastings Cutoff. The difference may be accounted for if one considers that it is doubtful that the rear wheels of the wagon creating the ruts followed precisely in the tracks of the front wheels. Comparison of the ruts from sites 42T0468, 42To469, the Great Salt Lake Desert running gear, and the Oregon Trail wagons suggests that the ruts were made by light farm wagons (Figure 76).

The ruts from site 42To467 vary drastically from the wheel spacings for the Oregon wagons as well as from the ruts from the other sites. These ruts measure 10 inches wide at the base and are spaced 86 inches apart. The spacing is either too wide or too narrow to be explained by any of the twentieth-century vehicles known to have visited the sites. Site stratigraphy suggests that the ruts were made prior to 1850 at a time contemporaneous with the ruts at the other sites. The most logical explanation for the ruts at 42To467, and the explanation most in keeping with the historical record, is that they were produced by James Reed's Pioneer Palace. While there is no record of this wagon's dimensions which can be used for comparison, such a conclusion seems reasonable. If so, it appears that no wagon was abandoned at the site since Reed is known to have salvaged the vehicle after returning from a camp in the Pilot Range. The abandoned wheel and the large hole dug into the playa along one rut may well be associated with this salvage effort. The large array of domestic goods and the absence of any evidence of a wagon body is in keeping with Reed's story of salvaging his Palace and caching everything but provisions, bedding, and clothing. The archaeological evidence casts doubt on Virginia Reed's reminiscences, since it is clear that no wagons were buried in holes. The "cache" that James Reed reportedly made must, at most, have been a very simple one, consisting only of his family's goods stacked together on top of the playa. The orientation of the artifacts across the desert surface and stratigraphically below the wind-blown sand which covers the site suggest that Reed's cache was disturbed relatively soon after he abandoned it.

The orientation of the ruts encountered at sites 42To467, 42To468, and 42To469 varies from 54 degrees west of north at 42To467 to 63 degrees west of north at 42To469. These bearings lead one from site to site. The ruts followed during the 1987 reconnaissance lead to site 42To467 and continue northwest from site 42To470. The association of artifacts from the 1840s with these ruts, and their relationship to sites 42To467–471, suggests that the route followed in 1986 and illustrated in Figure 74 was at least one of the routes traveled by emigrants across the mud flats of the Great Salt Lake Desert. There may, in fact, be several more wagon track routes that we did not identify, since, in all probability, there was no one route across the salt flats even at the time of the Donner-Reed trek. With the passage of each succeeding vehicle, it becomes increasingly difficult to get through the mud of the flats, and it seems highly likely that the wagons may have been following individual routes and/or traveling side by side across the desert. The lack of multiple ruts at any of the excavated sites supports such a reconstruction.

The mythology surrounding the Donner-Reed saga contains, as a substantial component, stories of large caches of goods, including gold and other precious objects, buried by the party in the desert. While this is the stuff of which good legends are made, both the historical record and the archaeological data suggest it just was not so. Most of these legends appear to be based on Virginia Reed Murphy's account of buried caches and on trapper Fallon LeGros's story that he recovered gold and jewelry from Donner-Reed party cabin sites at

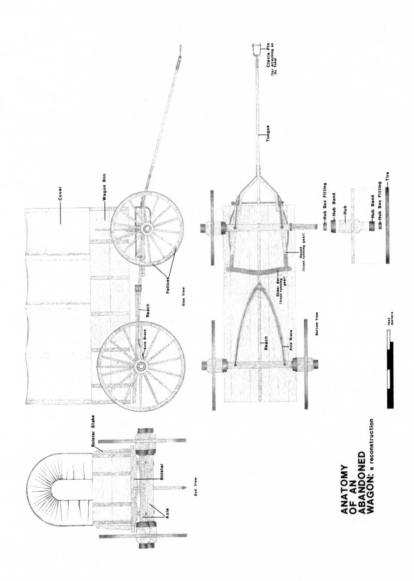

Figure 76. Reconstruction of a typical light farm wagon probably used by the Donner-Reed party.

Donner Lake (Stewart 1936). However, since Murphy's reminiscences were based on secondhand information and were written well after the fact, they must be considered suspect. Furthermore, if LeGros's tale has any degree of accuracy, any precious metals and gems were apparently carried at least as far as the Sierras and were not left in the desert. We do know that a cache of gold coins was found at Donner Lake in the late nineteenth century, adding support to LeGros's story and further suggesting no gold was left on the salt flats (Hardesty 1988 personal communication).

While both wagons and domestic goods were clearly abandoned at the sites, there is no evidence that any attempt was made to bury them in a cache for later retrieval. Direct historical records from other participants are mute on the subject, but the journals of Stansbury and others contain no indication that they passed buried mounds of earth. Given the visual environment of the salt flats – an absolutely featureless plain where at great distances even the smallest object stands out like Mount Fujiyama – such an omission speaks loudly against the presence of buried caches.

The only "mounds" on the salt flats are those associated with the wagon sites found or described by a number of expeditions. The most well documented is that of Charles Kelly who described the remains of five wagons which his 1929 expedition observed on the mud flats of the Great Salt Lake Desert. Photographs from the expedition show two sites with landmarks containing wagon remains. The landmark positions from these photographs match those observed and photographed from sites 42To468 and 42To469. Photographs from a third site show wagon wheel hubs in positions which suggest that a wagon collapsed at that site. Wagon parts from sites 42To469, 42To470, and 42To471 suggest that at least one wagon was abandoned at each of these sites. Yet nothing was encountered at any of the sites to suggest that the abandoned wagons or their contents were buried. To the contrary, in all the early photographs, wagon parts are well exposed and are only lightly covered at their bases (e.g., Figures 5, 7, and 8). This is consistent with the archaeological data which indicates that domestic goods and the bones of dead oxen and horses/mules were strewn across an undisturbed playa surface and then covered with wind-blown sand. There are, in short, no man-made "mounds" of cached goods, but rather the wagon sites consist of low dunes created by objects on the playa surface trapping wind-blown sand. The mounds were self-made through a natural process.

Given the number of people who crossed the desert muds during the middle of the nineteenth century, we are not altogether positive just who abandoned the wagons at the sites investigated by the Silver Island Expedition. Journals, travelers' accounts, and other documents record that 17 groups of emigrants, soldiers, and explorers traveled across Hastings Cutoff between 1846 and 1850. Of these, two groups are known to have abandoned wagons on the mud flats of the Great Salt Lake Desert – the Donner-Reed party abandoned four wagons in 1846 and the John Wood party left one wagon in 1850. If no additional unknown and unrecorded parties used Hastings Cutoff and if the extant records of the known groups accurately reflect all wagon abandonments, then a minimum of four of the five wagons can be accounted for on the basis of observations made by Kelly in 1929 and of the material recovered in 1986. At least three abandoned wagons are represented by sites 42To468–471 and a fourth existed at a site near the "Birds Nests" in Section 23, Township 1 North, Range 14 West. Site 42To467 most likely represents goods from James Reed's salvaged wagon, but it is also quite possible that a fifth wagon was also abandoned at the site and that the ruts it left lie undetected outside our excavation area. It seems even more likely that 42To469 represents the remains of more than one wagon and that all five wagons known to be abandoned can be accounted for.

For the most part, determining which of the sites represent the remains of the Donner party's wagons and which represent the remains of Wood's wagon is entirely speculative. However, the activities represented by the remains at site 42To469 suggest that this site may contain the remains of one or more Donner party wagon. A large concentration of charcoal and the remains of charred planks in a 9-by-3-foot area of the site suggest that a significant quantity of wood was burned there. Given the location and the unlikely probability that such a large amount of wood would have been hauled out onto the salt flats for a bivouac or a barbecue, it seems most probable that the burned wood is from abandoned wagons and/or numerous articles of furniture. The scattered remnants of broken wagon parts and wood fragments also suggest that one or more wagons were dismantled at this site and burned for firewood. There are two reasonable possibilities as to who was responsible.

Captain James Brown's detachment of Mormon Battalion soldiers and Captain Howard Stansbury's party of government explorers are the only recorded parties to have burned abandoned wagons on the mud flats of the Great Salt Lake Desert. Brown's detachment burned at least two wagons for firewood at one site while camped on the desert in 1847 en route to Salt Lake City from Sutter's Fort, California. Stansbury's party burned an "ox yoke, part of an old barrel, and part of an old wagon bed" while camped on the desert in 1849 en route to Salt Lake City following their circumnavigation of the Great Salt Lake. Since none of the other sites contained charcoal in sufficient quantities that could account for the burning of an ox yoke and wagon(s), it is possible that both parties camped at the same site. The presence of military buttons, a military musket cap, and a .64-caliber musket ball suggest that a party with military equipment visited 42To469, but whether the equipment belonged to Stansbury's party, Brown's detachment, or represents surplus material purchased by an emigrant at auction is unknown. Of the three possibilities, use of the site by Stansbury and his men seems to be substantiated the most. Geological specimens at the site are from source areas in the Promontory, Raft River, and Pilot mountains of northern Utah, and Stansbury's group is the only one on record that traveled east over Hastings Cutoff after having visited these ranges.

If Stansbury's and Brown's parties were responsible for the charcoal concentrations at site 42To469 and if Wood's party of immigrants did not cross the cutoff until 1850, then only the Donner-Reed party or an unknown emigrant party could have been responsible for the abandonment of wagons and oxen at this site. While horse/mule bones and dung were recovered from this site, and both Brown and Stansbury's party utilized mules for transportation, neither mentions a loss of animals on the mud flats. The Donner-Reed party apparently had mules (Hardesty 1987), but there is no record of their losing any on the salt flats, and it may well be that one of the numerous parties of emigrants utilizing pack animals also encountered trouble at this site while crossing Hastings Cutoff.

Sites 42To467 and 469 appear to have remained "relatively" undisturbed by previous expeditions. Smaller artifacts, separated from the surface of the mud flats by a thin layer of sand, appear to be randomly scattered across both sites. Areas of heaviest concentration are near wagon-related features. This distribution suggests that the abandoned wagons at these sites were systematically ripped apart and plundered within a relatively short time following their abandonment. The larger goods from the wagon cargo appear to have been looted, while smaller items and parts dropped or torn loose during the vandalism became randomly scattered across the sites. The absence of items observed by Stansbury in 1849 also suggests that many were carried off. Stansbury observed "innumerable articles of clothing, tools, chests, trunks, books & c . . . yokes, chains." Of these items, only four small remnants of fabric, ten buttons, eight tools, and two small parts to a chest or trunk were found during the 1986 investigations. Despite the number of twentieth-century expeditions and the large amount of loot they are known to have recovered, the lack of stratigraphy separating the artifactual remains from the surface of the mud flats suggests that most of the domestic items were carried off shortly after the wagons were abandoned. For example, during the spring of 1850, after hearing Stansbury's descriptions of the abandoned goods, Cyrus Call and Samuel Mecham of Tooele, Utah, were rumored to have gone to the wagon sites, recovered the abandoned goods, and returned with them to Salt Lake City (Kelly 1930:152). The *Deseret News* failed to report the event, however, and any number of other recovery attempts may have gone, and probably did go, unrecorded.

At 42To469, the large quantity of exploded or fired percussion caps that were recovered (13) requires some explanation. Only one other fired cap was recovered from the remaining sites. One possible explanation may be that they were used to kill the dying animals whose remains were found at the site. Thirteen shots to kill three dying animals would suggest that the emigrants doing the shooting were exceedingly poor shots, exceedingly drunk, or didn't know one end of a gun from the other. No expended rifle, musket, or pistol balls were associated with the animal remains. A second explanation may be that the caps were expended by Brown's detachment or Stansbury's party. Stansbury (1852a) refers to one occasion around the evening campfire when his celebrating French Canadians jubilantly fired their weapons blindly into the night. However, the conditions under which both groups camped during their night on the mud flats suggest that there was little to celebrate during their desert crossings. Following a quick cup of coffee, and a bit of warmth from a fleeting fire, the campers undoubtedly sought what little refuge their blankets had to offer. The third and most plausible alternative involves the fire that created the charcoal concentration. It seems entirely possible that a small box of percussion caps which may have remained in the wagon began to heat up, finally reaching the point of ignition for some of the caps. As the box exploded, fired and unfired caps alike were scattered to the locations from which they were found. The probability of this last alternative is supported by documentary evidence that the Donner-Reed party was using percussion weapons (e.g., Stewart 1936). However, archaeological evidence of weaponry from Murphy's cabin at Donner Lake, California, consists only of gunflints; no percussion caps were found (Hardesty 1987).

Many of the larger questions we hoped to investigate in conjunction with our study of the Hastings Cutoff sites cannot be investigated in isolation and must be explored in terms of other sites and sources of information. To explore the topic of emigrant wagon cargoes and their relationship to emigrant lifeways and traditions requires not only an inventory of the goods with which they started their journey, but also a knowledge of the emigrant parties, their composition, backgrounds, and the localities and cultural systems of which they were a part. Such a study also assumes that provenience to a particular emigrant group can be assigned each site or item—an assumption that is only rarely valid. However, data useful in comparing the material culture of overland emigrant parties is limited largely to provenienced materials from museum collections.

We have discovered only three archaeological projects which involved emigrant sites from overland trails, and only two of these involved actual excavation, the other was simply an inventory of sites. As a result, many of our larger questions can be addressed only with difficulty. We are very fortunate, on the other hand, that one of these two archaeological investigations is directly related to the Hastings Cutoff wagon sites. Through what appears at first glance to be a marvelous coincidence, but on reflection is more probably due to the fame of the Donner story, excavations were conducted in 1984 and 1985 at one of the Donner-Reed party cabin sites in the Sierra (Hardesty 1987). Data from these excavations are comparable to our work and, when examined together with the Silver Island data, provide a more comprehensive picture of the material culture of one of the most prominent western emigrant parties.

The most striking feature of the two data sets is the similarity in the array of domestic goods found at the two sites. Material from 1872 "excavations" of the Donner Lake site reported by C. F. McGlashan (1880) and the 1984 and 1985 excavations of Murphy's cabin, such as decorated whiteware china, green salt-glazed stoneware, cobalt blue medicine bottles, etc., are very similar to related items from along Hastings Cutoff. Given that these items were deposited by the same group of people, all of whom were from essentially the same area and who shared relatively similar backgrounds, such a pattern is not unexpected. Perhaps more surprising is the relatively broad array of goods that are represented and the insight that this array gives us into the life-styles of this group. Even after nearly 150 years of looting, curio hunting, and "excavation," material culture remains at the two sites are strongly consonant with documentary evidence that these were relatively affluent people. Even without the historical record, the list of goods from virtually every domestic category is suggestive of well-stocked households with everything from dinner plates to carpenter's tools to medicinal supplies to hunting gear to items of personal decoration. Clearly, the people who left these remains were not poor indigent farmers.

The nature of the remains at the Donner Lake sites provides grist for speculation as to who may have been responsible for some of the domestic goods scattered along Hastings Cutoff. As a result of the limited kinds of material goods at Murphy's cabin, Hardesty (1987:264) notes that there is a marked difference in the number and kind of domestic artifacts at the Donner Lake sites, and that there were "some real differences in the artifacts brought by the occupants of the three cabins, perhaps reflecting personal ideas about the value of things such as dishes and kitchen utensils." Perhaps—but an equally reasonable argument can be made that the reason there are so few domestic goods in that California mountain cabin is because they were strewn throughout the Utah deserts. While only Reed, Donner, and Keseberg are known to have lost wagons, it is clear that they and others were "lightening" their loads well before the wagons were abandoned. It seems plausible that the Murphys, Eddys, and Fosters were also forced to leave domestic goods on the mud flats to ease the strain on their overburdened animals. As noted earlier, the Eddy family was particularly destitute after their bout with the Great Salt Lake Desert, and it seems just as probable that the lack of domestic artifacts at Murphy's cabin is less the result of personal ideas than of necessity and circumstance.

There are a number of differences between the Hastings Cutoff sites and the Donner Lake sites which are telling. One major difference is that no beads, brooches, or other baubles appear to have been discarded in the desert, while at Donner Lake personal ornaments constitute one of the most common recognizable artifact types. Despite the relic hunting which has occurred at the sites, given the array of small items on the salt flats, we would expect to find at least some evidence of personal ornaments had they been left there. Apparently, jewelry, real or costume, was a highly curated item. So too, were tobacco pipes; at Murphy's cabin, clay pipe fragments are the second most common identified artifact, while none were recovered from the wagon sites along Hastings Cutoff. While it is interesting to speculate that it is easier on the psyche to discard a scrub brush or a carpenter's auger than it is to throw away an earring heirloom or a favorite pipe, an alternate explanation is that these personal items constituted such a small part of the load that they really added little to the cost of transporting goods beyond the Utah deserts.

Given the number and variety of weapons evident at both the Donner Lake and Hastings Cutoff sites, it appears that the Donner-Reed party was supplied with a veritable arsenal of rifles, muskets, shotguns, and pistols. Both the weapons themselves and the projectiles they shot were recovered from both locations, and apparently there were enough weapons in the party that it was possible to abandon some and still have enough for both hunting and protection.

Over all, the first efforts at archaeological excavation of materials left along the California and Oregon trails are beginning to shed some light on the nature of westering emigrant parties. While initial studies, such as our own along Hastings Cutoff and that of Donald Hardesty's at Donner Lake, have focused on what is probably the most famous emigrant group, other future historical archaeological projects should continue to flesh out the wider picture. As this library of materially oriented studies grows, it should begin to substantially supplement and even modify the existing written record. In the case of the saga of the Donner-Reed party, probably one of the best documented of all western emigrant stories, it is clear that written source material is often less accurate and less reliable than physical remains. Even the written records of careful scientists such as Howard Stansbury are possible sources of error—his journal, for example, records four wagons his party passed in the night while his published version describes five. On the other hand, it would probably be impossible to disentangle the material record at complex sites like 42To469 without documentary evidence such as Stansbury's journal and James Reed's diary. Clearly, the two types of data must be used in concert to reconstruct actual events and circumstances. By combining archaeological studies with the existing written record, our understanding of the settling of the West will be substantially enhanced. The archaeological investigation of Donner-Reed wagons abandoned along Hastings Cutoff is a step in that direction.

Textile and Brush Analysis

Ann Hanniball

*T*he fragments of four textiles, a small leather knot, a complete shaving brush, a bristle sample from a scrub brush, and the fragmentary remains of two pieces of rope were recovered from sites 42To467 and 469. The analysis of this group of historic textiles was carried out at the Utah Museum of Natural History (UMNH) Collections Laboratory under the direction of Ann Hanniball. Jane Tomb, Kathy Kankainen, Becky Menlove, and Tina Burton also participated in the project. Drawings are by Kathy Kankainen and photomicrographs by Paul Trentelman and Ann Hanniball.

ANALYSIS PROCEDURE

A Wild M3z zoom stereoscope with a magnification range of 6.5X to 40X was used to make initial observations. More detailed microscopic examinations were made with a Zeiss (polarizing) Photomicroscope III. Arcolor 5442 (with a refractive index of 1.660) was the mounting medium that was used to make microslides. All observations were longitudinal, unless cross sectioning is explicitly mentioned in the text, and were made at magnifications of 250X and 625X. Fiber diameters were measured with an ocular micrometer. Photomicrographs were taken with Kodak Panatomic X film, ASA 32.

The nomenclature used to describe weave structures is from Emery (1980). Because it was not possible to distinguish warp from weft, horizontal and vertical directions were arbitrarily designated axis A and axis B. Specimen measurements were made with Mitutoyo calipers, or with a standard measuring tape, marked in centimeters. For thread dimension, three yarns (threads) per sample were measured; the range of measurements are listed. The term indigo in this text refers to the color, not necessarily to the dye derived from the plant *Indigofera* sp.

All of the samples were damp when they were delivered to the UMNH. They were also heavily coated with salt crystals and other soil deposits, so fiber samples were repeatedly rinsed in distilled water before microslides were made. If a single textile sample consisted of several separate pieces, all of the pieces were numbered and sampled, with the exception of 42To467 Sample #3 (Fs210). Several specimens were contained in bags of moist soil; these were extracted by placing the damp soil clumps between two polyester silkscreens and gently rinsing with a diffuse stream of water until the specimen was discernable. Further cleaning was carried out under the stereoscope with a metal needle probe and tweezers. Fiber contaminants were sampled and analyzed only when the original association with the textile specimen seemed absolutely firm. Burn tests were conducted on samples from all of the specimens and results are mentioned where pertinent.

TEXTILE DESCRIPTION
42To469 – Textile Sample #1 (Fs 127)

Thread count: 12 threads/cm along axis A (brown elements); 12–14 threads/cm along axis B (white elements).

Thread dimensions: Brown elements (axis A): 0.062–0.090cm; White elements (axis B): 0.038–0.046cm.

Number and material of elements: Two elements; S spun brown wool single yarns in the direction of axis A, and S spun white wool single yarns in the direction of axis B.

Weave structure: 2/1 twill. There is a symmetrical reversal near one end of the specimen. No selvedges are present (Figure 77a).

Sample #1 was initially composed of three lumps of damp, sandy soil, each containing textile fragments. These were numbered Sample #1a (Fs127.1), 1b (127.2), and 1c (127.3) at the UMNH. A fourth fragment, washed during preliminary artifact processing prior to being deposited at the museum, was numbered Sample #1d. Sample #1c was not washed. Sample #1a and 1d were recovered with a visible weave

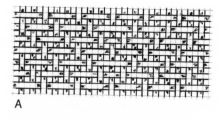
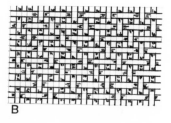

Figure 77. Weave structures in textile samples from 42To467 and 469: (a) Sample #1 (Fs127); (b) Sample #2a (Fs216.1).

structure; Sample #1b yielded an incoherent mass of brown and white S spun wool single yarns.

On initial examination, the brown elements in Sample #1 had a strong, lustrous, almost silky look and seemed significantly more stable than the white elements, which appeared to dissolve in water if touched with a needle or immersed for any length of time. The brown fibers had a very distinct mosaic imbricate scale pattern, with smooth scale margins. Scale spacing was fairly regular, at ca. 9.5-micron intervals. No medullae were observed. Dark spots, probably melanin bodies, were clearly visible (Textile Institute 1975). The fibers were quite uniform in diameter size along their length, although there was a size range of 25 microns (from 15.0 to 40.0 microns) between the measured fibers. A high proportion of guard hairs was observed in each sample. Damage consisted of serrated or bitelike notches along the margins of the fibers as they were observed longitudinally; otherwise, the fibers were relatively intact (Figure 78a).

The fragile, disarticulated, broken appearance of the white elements in Sample #1 could be observed both without and with magnification. The scale pattern was very difficult to see and was visible only in the semitransparent cuticle or epicuticle, which occasionally still surrounded the shattered, needlelike, elliptical cortical tissue (Morton and Hearle 1975; Mauersberger 1948). No medullae were observed. Fiber sizes were difficult to determine because of extensive damage; measured fibers ranged from 16.8 microns to 18.7 microns, with scales at ca. 9.5-micron intervals. The very degraded and disintegrated condition of the white as compared to the brown elements of Sample #1 (Figure 78b), suggests that the white wool had been chemically treated (possibly bleached) at some time (Mauersberger 1948).

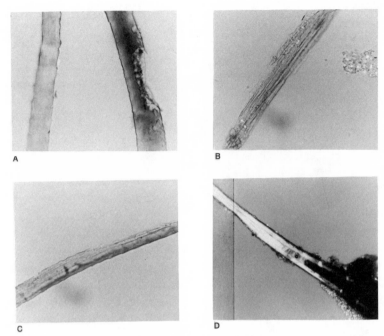

Figure 78. Photomicrographs of textile fragments from 42To469: (a) Sample #1a (Fs127.1) [brown] (625x); (b) Sample #1a [white] (625x); (c) Sample #2a (Fs216.1) (625x); (d) Sample #2b (Fs216.2) (625x).

42To469 – Textile Sample #2a (Fs 216.1)

 Dimensions: L: 4.0cm, W: 4.5cm. Two small fragments (L: 2.3cm, W: 1.0cm and L: 1.8cm, W: 0.9cm) were loosely attached to the larger specimen.

 Thread count: 12-13 threads/cm along the direction of axis A, 14-15 threads/cm along the direction of axis B.

 Thread dimensions: Axis A: 0.046-0.050cm.; Axis B: 0.048-0.050cm.

 Number and material of elements: Two elements. Both axis A and axis B are composed of Z spun dark blue wool single yarns and slightly Z or unspun brown wool fibers.

 Weave structure: 2/1 twill. No selvedges are present (Figure 77b). The two elements lie parallel to each other in both directions and were probably once combined, but have mostly separated, perhaps during or after finishing processes (such as washing, fulling, or brushing).

Sample #2a was composed of three loosely attached fragments of a dark blue, possibly napped, textile. Another, detached fragment of different composition, Sample #2b (Fs216.2), was recovered with #2a and delivered to the UMNH in the same storage container. The brown elements of #2a appeared to "float," predominately on one surface of the textile, as a largely disorganized, seemingly unspun nap. At 250X, the brown fibers looked featureless, flattened and ribbonlike. Examination at higher magnification (625X) revealed scales, primarily visible as regular ridges along the fiber margins, at approximately 9.5-micron intervals. No medullae were observed. Many of the damaged fibers were longitudinally split or broken, although not with sufficient consistency to explain their flattened appearance. This may have occurred as a result of finishing processes (Figure 78c).

The blue elements in Sample #2a were extremely brittle, and broke into small particles when they were touched with a needle or transferred to a microslide. At both 250X and 625X, the fibers appeared as disorganized bundles of rodlike elements, sometimes with pointed ends. Because the blue fibers reacted like burning hair to heat and flame, it seems probable that they are wool, so modified and damaged by dyeing and finishing processes, and by the alkaline environment of 42To469, that only separated cortical tissue remains (Textile Institute 1975; Mauersberger 1948).

42To469 – Textile Sample #2b (Fs216.2)
    Dimensions: L: 1.8cm, W: 1.0cm.
    Number and material of elements: One element; worked hide.
    Structure: Simple knot (?)
    Sample #2b is a dark blue hide fragment, possibly deliberately knotted, and dotted with short, abruptly tapered, rodlike hairs with a closely spaced mosaic or wave scale pattern. Continuous, abruptly tapering medullae terminate at a flat, possibly cut, distal end. Medullae are irregular in outline (erose) in the basal region and become simple and unbroken near the tip (Figure 78d). A single bright blue cotton fiber was found lying on the surface of this specimen, beneath an encrusted salt layer.

42To467 – Sample #3 (Fs210)
    Thread count: 26-30 threads/cm along the direction of axis A,
        24 threads/cm along the direction of axis B.

Thread dimensions: Axis A: 0.034-0.035cm, axis B: 0.021-0.022cm.

Number and material of elements: Two elements. Z spun indigo blue wool single yarns in the direction of axis A; unidentified material in the direction of axis B.

Weave structure: 2/1 twill. No selvedges are present.

A large number of shredded blue textile fragments, generally with a long, narrow shape and a maximum size of 0.75cm by 2.0cm, were delivered to the museum in a washing screen. All are pieces of the same textile, a finely woven blue twill composed of Z spun wool single yarns in the direction of axis A, invariably the long axis, and an unidentified material in the other, short, B direction. The wool fibers had a flattened, featureless appearance. Scales were difficult to see; a faint mosaic pattern with apparently smooth scale margins at ca. 7.5-micron intervals was discernable. There were no visible medullae. The most obvious damage consisted of jagged breaks along the fiber margins.

On initial examination, the unidentified material looked flat, ribbonlike, and densely colored. Very little of it was extant. It shattered into tiny particles on contact. It proved impossible to create sections thin enough to transmit light.

42To467 – Textile Sample #4 (Fs233)

Dimensions: L: 47.0cm, W: 25.0cm (2 pieces joined by a seam).

Thread count: 21 threads/cm along the direction of axis A (long axis), 21 threads/cm along axis B (short axis).

Thread dimensions: Axis A: 0.011-0.027cm; axis B: 0.022-0.030cm.

Number and material of elements: Three elements. Z spun indigo blue wool single yarns along axis A; S spun indigo blue wool single yarns along axis B; Z spun 2-ply S twist light brown silk thread along one extant seam section.

Weave structure: 1/1 balanced plain weave. One face of this specimen has a napped or felted surface. No selvedges are present.

Accessory structures: There is a 14.7cm section of backstitched seam.

Sample #4 is an irregularly shaped piece of textile, with some edges that appear to have been cut. The specimen is in two pieces; a large piece joined to a much smaller, narrow fragment by a section of seam sewn with silk thread in an irregular running stitch at measured intervals of 0.11 to 0.30cm. Both pieces are folded at the seam. Two round holes, 1.0cm and 1.3cm in diameter, are located next to each other, near an edge. There are also three irregular tears in the textile. The deep indigo blue color of this specimen is very fugitive and is easily transferred in water to blotting paper.

Both the S and Z spun wool exhibited a very flattened and featureless appearance at both 250X and 625X. Scales were discernable only as faint ridges, at regular 7.5-micron intervals along the edges of the fibers. No medullae were visible, but multiple longitudinal striations were observed along the length of the fibers. Measured fibers ranged in size from 15.5 to 18.5 microns in the wide dimension of the flattened ribbonlike shape. The fibers reacted like burning hair to a flame and heat; their microscopic appearance is similar to some samples of fulled or felted wool. Typical flattened crossover marks could be observed in the silk fibers, which also exhibited the optical properties of silk in polarized light. Measured fibers ranged in size from 9.5 to 13 microns. Fibers were relatively undamaged and did not appear to have been dyed.

BRISTLE DESCRIPTION

42To469 — Brush Sample #1 (Fs135)

> Dimensions: #1a (Fs135.1) L: 2.9cm, W: 2.5cm; #1b (Fs135.2) L: 2.9cm, W: 1.8cm; #1c (Fs135.3) L: 3.6cm, W: 2.5cm; #1d (Fs135.4) L: 2.4cm, W: 2.9cm.
>
> Number and material of elements: One element; mammal hair (possibly *Sus* sp.)

Brush Sample #1 consisted of four separate groups of fibers, each bent at a sharp angle near their basal end to form an even clump. They were numbered 1a-1d (Fs135.1-135.4). All of the samples were coated with and/or attached to a dark, crumbly, woody material at their base, the point at which bristles would emerge from the surface of a brush handle. This material is undoubtedly derived from the wooden handle of the "scrub brush" recovered at 42To469 from which this sample was taken. (The handle was not delivered to the UMNH.)

All of the fibers had a dark band of pigment, of varying width, located midway between the proximal and the flagged distal ends.

Medullae were easily visible, and were continuous and circular to roughly star shaped in cross section. Measured fiber sizes ranged from 140 microns to 200 microns. A red cotton fiber was found tightly wound around a bristle in #1c.

42To469—Brush Sample #2 (Fs155)
    Dimensions: L: 6.9cm, W: 2.8cm.
    Number and material of fiber elements: One; mammal hair (possibly *Sus* sp.)
    Sample #2 is a shaving brush with bristles still attached to a horn base. The bristles were colorless, with ragged distal ends and continuous medullae. Their sizes ranged from 137 to 166 microns. They were stiff and brittle; outer fibers in the brush exhibited the most damage.

ROPE DESCRIPTION

An attempt was made to analyze two rope specimens from 42To469. The fragments were heavily impregnated with a thick, tarry, resinous material and were disarticulating, making detailed analyses virtually impossible. Little could be discerned beyond the fact that both fragments are composed of multiple plies of an unidentified plant material.

RESULTS

Three of the four textile samples are constructed of single-ply spun wool yarns. The remaining sample is composed of a single-ply wool in one direction and an unidentified element in the other. Three of the textiles are colored a deep indigo blue. Of these, one is a balanced plain weave with one felted or napped surface, one is a 2/1 twill, and one is a 2/1 twill with a nap of apparently undyed brown wool fibers. One of these blue fragments contained a section of seam sewn with plied silk thread. According to Todd et al. (1974), deep blue wool plain weave or twill broadcloth and twill kersey and "cassimere" (kerseymere?) fabrics were standard issue for U.S. military jackets between 1851 and 1872, and for trousers between 1858 and 1861. The fourth textile specimen is a 2/1 twill with a single reversal that is probably the remnant of a wave or zigzag pattern. It is constructed of brown (probably undyed) and white (probably chemically processed) wool. All of the wool elements were damaged, those which had apparently been chemically processed (dyed or bleached) most severely.

Mammal hairs from the two brushes were brittle and coated with salt, but are otherwise relatively intact. All of the hairs appear to be from the domestic pig (*Sus* sp.). The multiple-ply rope fragments were coated with tar. The only cotton found at the sites appeared as stray fibers, possibly contaminants, attached to two of the specimens.

Faunal Analysis

M. Elizabeth Manion

A total of 57 bones were identified from sites 42To467, 42To469, and 42To470 (Table 2). Identified fauna (35 percent of the collection) included *Bos/Bison*, *Equus*, and *Aves*. Large-mammal and unknown mammal bone accounted for 47 percent of the bone. An additional ten mud blocks were recovered with unidentifiable bone splinters (18 percent) embedded in them. An attempt was made to remove the bone from the dried mud, but the attempt proved destructively unsuccessful and was abandoned.

ANALYTICAL PROCEDURES

Vertebrate bones were identified by using the comparative faunal collections at the Division of State History and the Paleontological Collection at Brigham Young University. In addition, identifications were aided by a number of sources including Olsen (1973), Brown and Gustafson (1979), and by consultations with James Madsen, Jr., the Utah state paleontologist. An attempt was made to identify all faunal bone to the lowest taxonomic category of species. In addition to taxonomic identification, bones were analyzed for presence and degree of burning, presence/absence of cut marks, age, and condition.

With one minor exception, the identified bones were either *Equus* (horse/mule) or *Bos/Bison* (oxen/buffalo). However, in the latter instance Brown and Gustafson (1979:1) note the difficulty in distinguishing postcranial *Bos* (cow/oxen) from *Bison* (buffalo) bones. Because of this, and the lack of a large-mammal reference collection

TABLE 2. Faunal Remains

Site	Fs#	Vertebrate	Element	Age	Side	Comp	Cond
42To467	179–1	*Bos/Bison*	femur, maj troch	I	L		good
	179-2	*Bos/Bison*	vertebra	I			good
42To469	004-1	lg mammal	vert body ephysis	I			good
	004-2	lg mammal	vert body ephysis	I			good
	004-3	lg mammal	vert body ephysis	I			good
	004-4	lg mammal	long bone				excel
	004-5	lg mammal	long bone				excel
	004-6	lg mammal	long bone				good
	004-7	*Bos/Bison*	ectocuneiform	A	R	X	excel
	027-1	*Equus*	phalanx-first	A		X	excel
	029-1	*Bos/Bison*	phalanx-first	A		X	excel
	037-1	lg mammal	tarsal/carpal	A		X	excel
	037-2	lg mammal	tarsal/carpal	A		X	excel
	037-3	lg mammal	tarsal/carpal	A		X	poor
	072-1	mammal	bone splinters				poor
	076-1	mammal	bone splinters				poor
	076-2	mammal	bone splinters				poor
	076-3	mammal	bone splinters				poor
	076-4	mammal	bone splinters				poor
	076-5	mammal	bone splinters				poor
	076-6	mammal	bone splinters				poor
	076-7	mammal	bone splinters				poor
	077-1	*Bos/Bison*	phalanx-third			A	good
	112-1	lg mammal	bone fragment				poor
	114-1	unk	bone splinters				poor
	115-1	lg mammal	bone fragment				poor
	115-2	lg mammal	bone fragment				poor
	117-1	mammal	bone fragment				poor
	121-1	*Bos/Bison*	metatarsal	A	L		excel
	121-2	*Bos/Bison*	navico-cuboid	A	L	X	excel
	121-3	*Bos/Bison*	ectocuneiform	A	L	X	excel
	121-4	lg mammal	rib				poor
	121-5	lg mammal	rib				poor
	121-6	lg mammal	long bone				good
	125-1	*Bos/Bison*	phalanx-second	A		X	good
	126-1	lg mammal	long bone				good
	126-2	lg mammal	bone fragment				good
	136-1	*Equus*	radius/ulna	A	L	X	excel
	137-1	*Equus*	metacarpal	A	L		excel
	137-2	*Equus*	vest metacarpal	A	L		excel
	137-3	*Equus*	carpal	A	L	X	excel
	137-4	*Equus*	carpal	A	L	X	excel
	137-5	*Equus*	carpal	A	L	X	excel
	137-6	*Equus*	carpal	A	L	X	excel
	137-7	*Equus*	carpal	A	L	X	excel
	149-1	mammal	bone splinters				poor

TABLE 2. Faunal Remains (Continued)

Site	Fs#	Vertebrate	Element	Age	Side	Comp	Cond
42To470	174-1	Aves	phalanx	A			excel
	174-2	lg mammal	bone fragment				good
	176-2	lg mammal	vert tail				good
	177-1	lg mammal	rib				good
	178-1	*Bos/Bison*	vert-thoracic	I			good
	180-1	lg mammal	vert body ephysis	I			poor
	181-1	*Bos/Bison*	femur head ephysis	I	R		poor
	182-1	lg mammal	rib				poor

for oxen/cow/bison, the broad category of *Bos/Bison* was used in the analysis. There is, however, every indication from the available literature that the bones represent oxen rather than cows or bison. Supporting comparative analysis with the small bison collection at the Division of State History also suggests that the *Bos/Bison* bones derived from oxen. The same problem occurs with the *Equus* bones. Historical accounts indicate the presence of both horses and mules on Hastings Cutoff. Like the *Bos/Bison* dilemma, it is difficult to distinguish postcranial horse from mule bones, and the broad category of *Equus* was used in the analysis.

Animals and Sites

Site 42To469 contained the majority of the identified bone. Nine *Equus* and seven *Bos/Bison* elements were identified. The collection also includes 17 unidentifiable large mammals, and two mammal bone fragments. The remaining ten elements are so poorly preserved that they were recorded only as "bone splinters in mud." Identified elements are predominantly lower limb bones, vertebrae, and rib fragments. Six of the nine *Equus* elements represent the back left metacarpal/carpal complex of one individual. Three of the seven *Bos/Bison* elements are from the left forelimb of one individual. All *Bos/Bison* and *Equus* elements are from mature animals. The remains of a juvenile large mammal is represented by three vertebral body epiphyses. Generally, the bones from 42To469 are well preserved. This is not unusual as most of the bones are denser carpal/tarsal bones. The only exceptions are the bone splinters embedded in mud blocks. These may have been part of the less dense bone elements such as the interior skull.

Only nine bones were recovered from 42To470. The collection is composed primarily of vertebra body/tail elements and rib fragments. Only two bones could be identified to the genus level. Both bones are from a *Bos/Bison* juvenile. A horn core fragment and an *Aves* metacarpal are included with the 42To470 bone. The *Aves* metacarpal is believed to be incidental to this faunal collection.

Only two bones representing *Bos/Bison* were recovered from site 42To467. Both bones, a juvenile femur and a vertebral body, are well preserved.

DISCUSSION

At least five large mammals expired at sites 42To467, 469, and 470. At least three of these died at site 42To469 and included one horse or mule, one ox, and at least one additional juvenile large mammal. At both 42To467 and 42To470, it appears that at least one juvenile oxen died at the sites.

Site 42To469 is the most provocative because of the relatively large amount of bone. After traveling the route in the fall of 1849, Captain Howard Stansbury noted that "We passed during the night 4 wagons and one cart with innumerable articles of clothes, tool chest, trunks, books and c. yokes, chains and some half dozen dead oxen" (Madsen 1989). Based on this passage, one would assume that there should be more bone than was recovered at the sites. The number of individuals represented in the collection correlates well with Stansbury's observations, but an immediate question is raised as to why the rest of the bones are missing.

Horse, mule, and oxen have strong, dense bones obviously necessary to carry heavy burdens. One would think that most of the bones would survive. However, there are at least three obvious explanations indicating why they would not. One is the highly erosional quality of the salt flats. The repeated hydration and dehydration of salt crystals appears to be able to quickly erode away laminae at the surface of the bone and cause its eventual destruction. This possibility is indicated in the poorly preserved bone splinters in the mud blocks. The second explanation is the possibility that the animals were partially butchered and carried away for food. This may help explain the relatively high concentration of hock bones, especially at 42To469. These bones provide very little meat. A third explanation is heavy collection over the years. Collectors may have wanted a remembrance of their visit to the sites and rummaged around for a skull or a limb bone or whatnot.

(There are several references and museum collections believed to be from these sites. For example, an *Equus* mandible, distinctively horse, was located at the Grantsville Museum and was noted as being from the West Desert.) A combination of the first and third explanation seem most likely especially in light of the erosional quality of the salt flats and the concrete evidence of long-term collection. As there were no burn marks nor discernable cut marks on the bone and no written documentation of starvation among the various parties traveling through Hastings Cutoff, it would seem highly unlikely that the second explanation is the cause of the lack of bone.

The fauna recovered from the Donner-Reed sites along Hastings Cutoff contrast markedly with those from the Donner-Reed sites near Donner Lake (Hardesty 1987). Only 57 bones were recovered from all the Hastings Cutoff sites, while 306 were recovered from Murphy's Cabin. There is some similarity in that the largest percentage of identified bone from both locations is from *Bos/Bison*, but the number and kind of other faunal types differs markedly. Unlike Murphy's Cabin, there are no nondomestic animals from the Utah sites, and the bone is undamaged by cultural action such as marrow extraction. The second highest percentage of identified bone from the Hastings Cutoff locations is *Equus*, but only one horse/mule bone was recovered from Murphy's Cabin. It is possible that this difference can be attributed to the presence of other parties at the sites in the Great Salt Lake Desert.

CONCLUSION

In conclusion, the remains of at least five mammals were recovered from three of the excavated sites. At least one horse or mule, one adult and two juvenile oxen, and one additional juvenile large mammal were represented by the collection. The remains were of partial animals primarily derived from the lower limbs. Interpretative comparisons made between the archaeological data and written histories suggest that the fauna were most likely the remains of the various domestic animals used by emigrants traveling along Hastings Cutoff. Finally, this small collection indicates that from the age of the animals, the people who acquired them appear to have selected younger, stronger, and sturdier animals to make their journey to the promised land of California.

References

Abert, John J.
1849   Letter to Howard Stansbury, April 11, 1849. U.S. National Archives, War Department, Topographical Bureau, Letters Issued, II, October 13, 1848–September 15, 1849. Washington, D.C.

Adams, Charles F.
1981   *The Complete Guide to Blacksmithing, Horseshoeing, Carriage and Wagon Building and Painting.* Crown Publishers Inc. New York.

Andrews, Thomas Franklin
1970   The Controversial Career of Lansford Warren Hastings: Pioneer California Promoter and Emigrant Guide. PhD. dissertation. University of Southern California.
1973   Lansford W. Hastings and the Promotion of the Salt Lake Desert Cutoff: A Reappraisal. *The Western Historical Quarterly* 4:133–50.

Anonymous
n.d.   *Salt Lake City Directory and Classified Business Directory.* R. L. Polk Company. Salt Lake City.
1850   *Deseret News.* July 27, 31, and August 10, 1850.
1888   *Appleton's Cyclopaedia of American Biography.* D. Appleton & Co. New York.
1975   *Who Was Who in American History — The Military.* Marquis. Chicago.
1980   *Illustrated Catalogue of American Hardware of the Russell*

and Erwin Manufacturing Company. 1865 edition. 1980 facsimile edition. Association for Preservation Technology.

Barber, Danile M., and George R. Hamell
    1971   The Redware Pottery Factory of Alvin Wilcox at Mid 19th Century. *Historical Archaeology* 5:18–37.

Belden, Josiah
    1930   Historical Facts on California. *Utah Historical Quarterly* 3:55.

Bidwell, John
    1890   The First Emigrant Train to California. *Century* 41:106–30.

Billington, Ray Allen
    1956   *The Far Western Frontier.* Harper & Bros. New York.

Blackburn, Abner
    n.d.   Reminiscences. MS on file, Utah State Historical Society (A-307). Salt Lake City.

Blake, James
    1850   Letters in the *Sacramento Transcript.* October 14, 15, and November 2, 1850. Sacramento.

Booth, Andrew G.
    1860   *Notes on Biography of Cpt. John W. Gunnison, Formerly 1st Lieut. of the U.S.A., Goshen, Sullivan County, New Hampshire.* MS on file with the Huntington Library. Los Angeles.

Branstner, Mark
    1986   Ceramics. In B. R. Hawkins and R. B. Stamps, "Report of the Preliminary Excavations at Fort Gratiot 1814–1879 in Port Huron, Michigan." MS on file with the Museum of Arts and History, Port Huron, Michigan.

Brown, H. P., A. J. Panshin, and C. C. Forsaith
    1949   *Textbook of Wood Technology, Vol. 1.* McGraw-Hill Book Company, Inc. New York.

Brown, C. L., and C. E. Gustafson
    1979   A Key to Postcranial Skeletal Remains of Cattle/Bison, Elk, and Horse. *Reports of Investigations, No. 57.* Laboratory of Anthropology, Washington State University, Pullman.

Bryant, Edwin
    1848   *What I Saw in California.* D. Appleton & Co. New York.

Carrington, Albert
    1850–51   Journal. On file, Daughters of the Utah Pioneers. Salt Lake City.

Chiles, J. B.
    1930   A Visit to California in Early Times. *Utah Historical Quarterly* 3:53.

Chittenden, Hiram Martin
    1902   *The American Fur Trade of the Far West.* The Press of the Pioneers. New York.

Christy, Howard O.
    1978   Open Hand and Mailed Fist: Mormon-Indian Relations in Utah, 1847–52. *Utah Historical Quarterly* 46:220–27.

Cushion, J. P.
    1980   *Handbook of Pottery and Porcelain Marks.* Faber and Faber. London/Boston.

DeVoto, Bernard
    1943   *The Year of Decision: 1846.* Little, Brown & Co. Boston.

———, ed.
    1953   *The Journals of Lewis and Clark.* Houghton Mifflin. Boston.

Doggett, John, Jr., & Co.
    1844–50   *Doggett's New York City Directory.* New York.

Drury, Clifford M.
    1937   *Marcus Whitman, M.D.: Pioneer and Martyr.* The Caxton Printers, Ltd. Caldwell, Idaho.

Emery, Irene
    1980   *The Primary Structure of Fabrics.* The Textile Museum. Washington, D.C.

Emory, William H.
    1848   *Notes of a Military Reconnaissance from Fort Leavenworth, in Missouri, to San Diego, in California.* Government Printing Office. Washington, D.C.

Fairbanks, Merwin
    1962   Expedition Mirage: Relics, Mystery Mark Old Trail. *Deseret News and Telegraph* 358(42):B-1,4.

Fike, Richard E.
    1987   *The Bottle Book.* Peregrine Smith Books. Salt Lake City.

Frémont, John C.
    1843   *Report on an Exploration of the Country Lying between the Missouri River and the Rocky Mountains, on the Line of the Kansas and Great Platte Rivers.* Government Printing Office. Washington, D.C.
    1845   *Report of the Exploring Expedition to the Rocky Mountains in*

the year 1842, and to Oregon and North California in the years 1843–1844. Government Printing Office. Washington, D.C.

Goetzmann, William H.
1959 *Army Exploration in the American West, 1803–1863.* Yale University Press. New Haven.

Gram, John M.
n.d. Identification of Nineteenth-Century Glazed Earthenwares: Comments and Bibliography. Unpublished manuscript on file at the archaeology laboratory, Oakland University, Rochester, Michigan.

Gunnison, John W.
1843 U.S. Congress, Senate, Ex. Doc., Vol. 2, No. 5, 27th Cong., 3rd sess., serial no. 413, 289. Washington, D.C.
1852 *The Mormons.* Lippincott, Grambo & Co. Philadelphia.

Hardesty, Donald L.
1987 The Archaeology of the Donner Party Tragedy. *Nevada Historical Quarterly* 30: 246–68.

Hastings, Lansford W.
1845 *The Emigrants' Guide to Oregon and California.* George Conclin. Cincinnati.

Heath, Steven H.
n.d. Biographical Sketch of Albert Carrington. MS on file (Acc. 32). Marriott Library. University of Utah.

Horn, Huston
1974 *The Pioneers.* Time Life Books. New York.

Kelly, Charles
1930 *Salt Desert Trails.* Western Printing Co. Salt Lake City.
1936 *Old Greenwood.* Salt Lake City: Western Printing Co.
1952a Gold Seekers on the Hastings Cutoff. *Utah Historical Quarterly* 20:3–30.
1952b The Journal of Robert Chalmers. *Utah Historical Quarterly* 20:30–55.

Korns, J. Roderick
1951 West from Fort Bridger. *Utah Historical Quarterly* 19:1–297.

Lewis, Berkeley R.
1956 *Small Arms and Ammunition in the United States Service.* Smithsonian Institution. Washington, D.C.

Luscomb, Sally C.
    1967   *The Collector's Encyclopedia of Buttons.* Crown Publishers Inc. New York.

McCrone, Walter C., John Gustav Delly, and Samuel James Palenik
    1979   *The Particle Atlas,* vols. II, IV, and V. Ann Arbor Science Publishers. Ann Arbor.

McGlashan, Charles Fayette
    1880   *History of the Donner Party: A Tragedy of the Sierra.* H. S. Crocker Co. Sacramento.

Madsen, Brigham D., ed.
    1981   *A Forty-niner in Utah with the Stansbury Exploration of Great Salt Lake: Letters and Journal of John Hudson, 1848–50.* University of Utah Press. Salt Lake City.
    1989   *Exploring the Great Salt Lake: The Stansbury Expedition of 1849–1850.* University of Utah Press. Salt Lake City.

Malone, Dumas, ed.
    1935   *Dictionary of American Biography.* Charles Scribner's Sons. New York.

Mathews, J. Merrit
    1913   *Textile Fibers.* 3rd ed. John Wiley & Sons. New York.

Mattes, Merrill J.
    1969   *The Great Platte River Road.* Nebraska State Historical Society. Lincoln.

Mauersberger, Herbert R., ed.
    1948   *Mathews Textile Fibers.* 5th ed. John Wiley & Sons. New York.

Miller, David E.
    1958   The Donner Road Through the Great Salt Lake Desert. *Pacific Historical Review* 27:39–44.

Montgomery, R. T.
    1930   Narrative of Charles Hopper, a California Pioneer of 1841. *Utah Historical Quarterly* 3:54.

Morgan, Dale L.
    1943   *The Humboldt: Highroad of the West.* Farrar & Rinehart Inc. New York.
    1953   *Jedediah Smith and the Opening of the West.* Bobbs-Merrill. Indianapolis.

——, ed.
    1963   *Overland in 1846.* Talisman Press. Georgetown.

Morton, W. E., and J. W. S. Hearle
　　1975　　*Physical Properties of Textile Fibers.* 2nd ed. The Textile Institute. Manchester.

Mumey, Nolie
　　1955　　*John Williams Gunnison (1812–1853), The Last of the Western Explorers, A History of the Survey through Colorado and Utah with a Biography and Details of His Massacre.* Artcraft Press. Denver.

Oliver, Elizabeth
　　1977　　*American Antique Glass.* Western Publishing Co. Racine.

Olsen, Stanley J.
　　1973　　Mammal Remains from Archaeological Sites – Part I, Southeastern and Southwestern United States. *Papers of the Peabody Museum of Archaeology and Ethnology, Vol. 56, No. 1.* Harvard University Press. Cambridge.

Russell, Carl P.
　　1978　　*Firearms, Traps and Tools of the Mountain Men.* University of New Mexico Press. Albuquerque.

Schubert, Frank N.
　　1980　　*Vanguard of Expansion: Army Engineers in the Trans-Mississippi, 1819–79.* Government Printing Office. Washington, D.C.

Sloan, Eric
　　1979　　*A Museum of Early American Tools.* Ballantine Books. New York.

Stansbury, Howard
　　1849　　Journal. Entry of Friday November 2, 1849. U.S. National Archives, War Department, Topographical Bureau. Washington, D.C.

　　1850　　Letter to Brigham Young, February 4, 1850. Journal History of the L.D.S. Church. L.D.S. Archives. Salt Lake City.

　　1851　　Letter to J. J. Abert, January 17, 1851. U.S. National Archives, War Department, Topographical Bureau, Register of Letters Received, IV, No. 68, Rec'd Jan. 20, 1851. Washington, D.C.

　　1852a　　*An Expedition to the Valley of the Great Salt Lake of Utah.* Lippincott, Grambo & Co. Philadelphia.

　　1852b　　Letter to J. J. Abert, June 1, 1852. U.S. National Archives, War Department, Topographical Bureau, Register of Letters Received, IV, No. 449. Washington, D.C.

Stewart, George R.
1936   *Ordeal By Hunger.* H. Holt & Co. New York.
1962   *The California Trail.* McGraw-Hill. New York.

Stookey, Walter M.
1950   *Fatal Decision.* Deseret Book. Salt Lake City.

Textile Institute
1975   *Identification of Textile Materials.* Manchester.

Todd, Frederick P., George Woodbridge, Lee Wallace, Jr., and Michael C. McAfee
1974   *American Military Equipage 1851–1872*, vol. I. Company of Military Historians. Providence.

Webb, Henry J.
1956   Retracing the Long Drive. *Western Humanities Review* 10:383–85.
1957   The Long Drive on Hastings Cutoff. *California Historical Society Quarterly* 36:57–62.
1958   The Long Drive Again: A Note. *Western Humanities Review* 12:97.
1963   The Last Trek Across the Great Salt Lake Desert. *Utah Historical Quarterly* 31:26–33.

Wells, Daniel H.
1850   Letter to Howard Stansbury, April 5, 1850. Journal History of the L.D.S. Church. L.D.S. Archives. Salt Lake City.

Worthington, Hamp
1930   Letter to Charles Kelly, May 31, 1930. Charles Kelly Papers, Utah State Historical Society. Salt Lake City.

Young, Brigham
1849   Letter to Amasa Lyman, September 5, 1849. Brigham Young Papers, reel 31, box 12, folder 13, Outgoing Correspondence, L.D.S. Archives. Salt Lake City.

Index